Faith First

huda

Faith First

A HANDBOOK ON ISLAMIC BELIEFS

Muftī Sirāj Uddīn

Under the supervision of
Shaykh Muftī Saiful Islām

JKN Publications

First Published in July 2021

ISBN: 978-1-909114-94-4

British Library Cataloguing in Publication Data
A catalogue record for this book is available from the British Library.

Publisher's Note:

Every care and attention has been put into the production of this book. If however you find any errors, they are our own, for which we seek Allāh's ﷻ forgiveness and the reader's pardon.

Published by:

JKN Publications
118 Manningham Lane
Bradford
West Yorkshire
BD8 7JF
United Kingdom

t: +44 (0) 1274 308 456 | w: www.jkn.org.uk | e: info@jkn.org.uk

Book Title: Faith First
Author: Mufti Sirāj Uddīn
Supervisor: Shaykh Mufti Saiful Islām

Printed by: Mega Print, Turkey

بسم الله الرحمن الرحيم

"In the Name of Allāh, the Most Beneficent,
the Most Merciful"

Contents

Foreword

All praise belongs to Allāh ﷻ. We praise Him, seek His assistance and forgiveness, believe in Him, and place our trust in Him. We seek His refuge from the evils of our selves and the consequences of our bad deeds. We testify that there is no god besides Allāh ﷻ, He is One, He has no partner, and we testify that Muhammad ﷺ is His slave and Messenger.

Īmān (faith in Allāh ﷻ) is the key to salvation. Without it, our actions have no value. Everything depends on the sincerity of faith. For this reason, the first of the five foundational pillars of Islām is the shahādah (the declaration of faith).

Correcting one's beliefs is the first and foremost stage of tazkiyah (spiritual purification). Imām Abul Qāsim al-Qushayrī رحمه الله states:

أَوَّلُ مَا يَجِبُ عَلَى الْعَبْدِ إِذَا سَلَكَ طَرِيْقَ الْعُبُوْدِيَّةِ: طَلَبُ قَدْرٍ مِّنَ الْعِلْمِ، يُصَحِّحُ بِهِ اعْتِقَادَهُ فِي التَّوْحِيْدِ

"A slave's first obligation when (starting to) tread the path of servitude is to seek enough knowledge with which he can correct his belief in monotheism."

Therefore, to ensure that we hold the correct beliefs regarding Allāh ﷻ and the Last Day and to make every effort to protect our faith from corruption is imperative.

This beautiful book presents the fundamental beliefs of Islām in a very simple yet concise manner, covering the essentials of the Islamic Faith. In my humble opinion, this handbook is ideal as a first read of the Islamic Creed, and suitable for English-speaking Muslims aged ten and above.

It is my earnest desire to see this book included in the syllabus of our makātib and madāris around the world, so that Muslims who are studying in the English language can have the chance to study the basics of Islamic Creed under the supervision of their local scholars.

I pray that Allāh ﷻ accepts the efforts of my colleague, Mufti Sirāj Sāhib, in rendering this service, as I pray that He makes it a means of great benefit and success for its readers and teachers. Āmīn.

(Shaykh Mufti) Saiful Islām

Principal, Jāmiah Khātamun Nabiyyeen, Bradford, UK
Chief Editor, Al-Mu'min Magazine
March 2021/Sha'bān, 1442

وَمَن يُؤْمِنۢ بِٱللَّهِ يَهْدِ قَلْبَهُۥ ۚ

"And whoever [truly] believes in Allāh, He shall guide his heart." (64:11)

Introduction

Faith in Islām

The Source of Our Religion

Allāh ﷻ gave us the religion of Islām in two forms:

1. The glorious Qur'ān: This is the final word of Allāh ﷻ to mankind, containing essential guidance in the form of laws, directions and historical accounts.
2. The Sunnah: This is the Religious Practice, formed by the statements, actions and approvals of the Prophet ﷺ, which serve to explain the Qur'ān in word and action.

Muslims turn to the Qur'ān and the Sunnah for all guidance.

The Messenger ﷺ received the Qur'ān and Sunnah from Allāh ﷻ, and mankind received them through him. Thus, we understand and act upon the Qur'ān in accordance with the teachings and practice of the Prophet ﷺ.

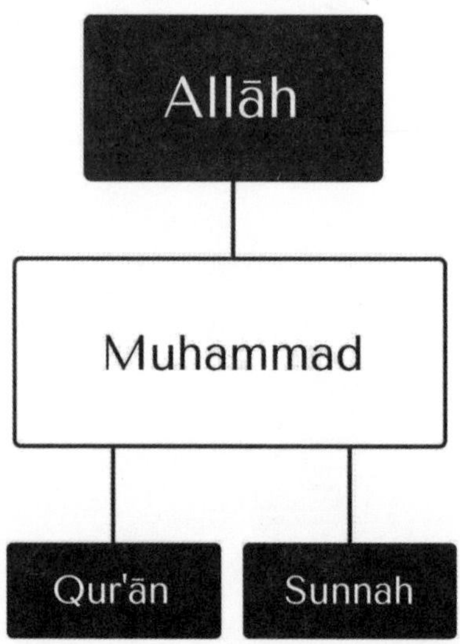

What is Faith

Īmān is the act of bringing faith in the fundamental beliefs of the religion of Islām. There are two essential components of Īmān:

1. Conviction: To hold an idea to be true in the heart.
2. Declaration: To profess the belief with the tongue.

1. Conviction

Allāh ﷻ says in the glorious Qur'ān:

﴿فَاعْلَمْ أَنَّهُ لَآ إِلٰهَ إِلَّا اللهُ﴾

"Know that there is no god besides Allāh." (47:19)

Īmān means to willingly accept the existence of Allāh ﷻ, His divinity, His unity, and His authority. It is to consciously believe that He alone is worthy of worship; He is unique; and He is in charge. This much knowledge (ma'rifah) is required to attain salvation in the Hereafter.

Since we can only know the correct beliefs through Allāh's ﷻ Messenger ﷺ, it is compulsory to bring faith in him too. Therefore, a Muslim must believe in the following statement:

لَآ إِلٰهَ إِلَّا اللهُ مُحَمَّدٌ رَّسُوْلُ اللهِ

'Lā ilāha ill-Allāh, Muhammadur Rasūlullāh.'

"There is no god but Allāh. Muhammad is Allāh's Messenger."

This statement is known by a few famous names:

1. Kalimat al-Islām (the Word of Islām)
2. Kalimat at-Tawhīd (the Word of Monotheism)
3. Kalimah Tayyibah (the Pure Word)

The Kalimah is comprehensive in that it necessarily includes all other tenets of faith and all that has come from Allāh ﷻ.

2. Declaration

When one has firmly internalised his faith in the above kalimah, one must pronounce it in the following way:

أَشْهَدُ أَنْ لَّا إِلٰهَ إِلَّا اللهُ وَأَشْهَدُ أَنَّ مُحَمَّدًا عَبْدُهٗ وَرَسُوْلُهٗ

'Ash-hadu al-lā ilāha ill-Allāh, wa ash-hadu anna Muhammadan 'abduhū wa rasūluh.'

"I testify that there is no god but Allāh ﷻ. And I testify that Muhammad ﷺ is His slave and Messenger."

- This is known as the Shahādah (the Declaration) and is the first and foremost pillar of Islām. It is an essential proof of one's faith. One's claim of being a Muslim can only be established and accepted in this world when one's belief in the Kalimah is followed by testimony.
- If a person refuses to declare his faith when required to do so (without a valid reason) then such a person is not considered a Muslim.

- The Shahādah allows one to identify as a Muslim and gives one the privilege of living and having one's affairs handled accordingly. Otherwise, there is no guarantee that one's affairs would be administered in accordance with Islamic Law. These include the following:
    i. Marriage
    ii. Burial and Funeral
    iii. Inheritance and Bequest
    iv. Court Testimony

The 5 pillars of

ISLĀM

Benefits of Faith

(1) Identity

Allāh ﷻ brought us into existence. Thus, we primarily identify ourselves as the slaves of Allāh ﷻ and believers in Him before anything else. All other forms of identity are secondary.

(2) Purpose

Islām gives us our purpose: to worship Allāh ﷻ and live in His service. We are aware that our fate in the Hereafter depends on our behaviour in this world. This allows us to be mindful of our behaviour and ensure that we live by His rules and regulations.

(3) Direction

Muslims trust Allāh ﷻ and rely on Him. He is the All-Knowing, the Wise. He loves and cares about us more than any of His creation does. That is why we turn to Allāh ﷻ with all our needs and seek His guidance and assistance in everything.

(4) Outlook

Islām tells us what life is truly about. It helps us put our life events into perspective and encourages us to prepare for the real life that lies ahead of us.

(5) Unity

Muslims are united by their belief in Allāh ﷻ. Islām gives us our code of life. We are one nation - we adhere to one set of laws, worship one God, and follow one Leader.

Faith: The Core of Human Behaviour

Belief is central to all aspects of human behaviour. It is the most powerful and significant of human behaviours and greatly influences how we think, feel and act.

Islām guides us in every aspect of our behaviour. The holy Prophet ﷺ provided us with complete guidance on how to achieve salvation, with faith always being first and foremost.

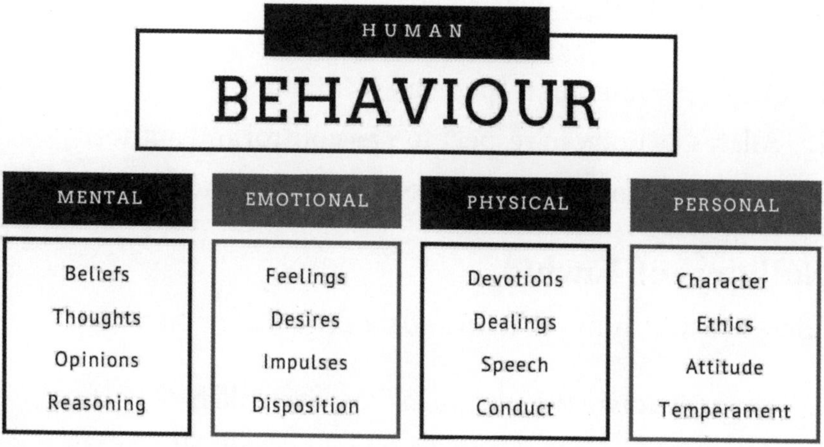

Our belief in Allāh ﷻ and the Hereafter keeps us conscious of right and wrong. It allows us to control our feelings and how we express them. It enables us to subdue the ego and work towards the betterment of our selves and society at large. It helps us make the right choices and behave in the right way. It also stops us from misusing our intelligence and free will.

Foundation of Faith

Tawhīd, or monotheism, is the most fundamental belief of Islām. It is the criterion of salvation and the central tenet of faith that connects all other tenets of faith to it. The glorious Qur'ān is dedicated to calling mankind towards tawhīd. For this reason, it is essential to understand its true meaning.

The Meaning of Tawhīd

Tawhīd means to believe in the unity (oneness) of Allāh ﷻ. His unity applies in three aspects:

1. Allāh's ﷻ unity in respect to His divinity.
2. Allāh's ﷻ unity in respect to His control and authority.
3. Allāh's ﷻ unity in respect to His essence and attributes.

Nullifiers of Tawhīd

There are two things that invalidate the belief of tawhīd:

1. **Kufr (atheism):** Kufr means to reject Allāh ﷻ i.e. to refuse to believe in Him: His existence, His authority, or His right to be worshipped and obeyed.
2. **Shirk (polytheism):** Shirk means to associate partners with Allāh ﷻ, consider others equal to Him in essence or attribute, or believe that His authority is shared.

Note: Kufr and shirk are both classed as the ultimate deviance. Should one die upon either, one dies with an unforgivable sin.

The Six Articles of Faith

The religion of Islām is based upon six fundamental articles of faith. To reject any of these articles is disbelief and takes one out of the fold of Islām .

They are as follows:

1. Belief in Allāh ﷻ.
2. Belief in His Angels.
3. Belief in His Scriptures.
4. Belief in His Messengers.
5. Belief in the Last Day.
6. Belief in Divine Decree.

We declare our faith in these articles in the following manner:

I believe in Allāh,	اٰمَنْتُ بِاللهِ،
His angels,	وَمَلَائِكَتِهٖ،
His Books,	وَكُتُبِهٖ،
His Messengers,	وَرُسُلِهٖ،
the Last Day,	وَالْيَوْمِ الْاٰخِرِ،
and in Divine Decree: the good and the bad.	وَالْقَدَرِ: خَيْرِهٖ وَشَرِّهٖ.

This set of beliefs is found in the following verses of the glorious Qur'ān:

﴿وَمَن يَكۡفُرۡ بِٱللَّهِ وَمَلَٰٓئِكَتِهِۦ وَكُتُبِهِۦ وَرُسُلِهِۦ وَٱلۡيَوۡمِ ٱلۡأٓخِرِ فَقَدۡ ضَلَّ ضَلَٰلَۢا بَعِيدًا﴾

"Whoever rejects Allāh, His angels, His Messengers, His Books, and the Last Day has indeed gone far astray." (4:136)

﴿لَّيۡسَ ٱلۡبِرَّ أَن تُوَلُّواْ وُجُوهَكُمۡ قِبَلَ ٱلۡمَشۡرِقِ وَٱلۡمَغۡرِبِ وَلَٰكِنَّ ٱلۡبِرَّ مَنۡ ءَامَنَ بِٱللَّهِ
وَٱلۡيَوۡمِ ٱلۡأٓخِرِ وَٱلۡمَلَٰٓئِكَةِ وَٱلۡكِتَٰبِ وَٱلنَّبِيِّـۧنَ﴾

"Piety is not in turning your faces towards the East or the West. Rather, true piety is that you believe in Allāh, the Last Day, the angels, the Scripture, and the Messengers." (2:177)

Note: The sixth article, namely the belief in qadar, is found in the well-known hadīth of Jibrīl عليه السلام and is supported by numerous verses of the glorious Qur'ān.

Hadīth of Jibrīl عليه السلام

It was narrated on the authority of Sayyidunā 'Umar ibn al-Khattāb رضي الله عنه, who said:

One day, while we were sitting with the Messenger of Allāh ﷺ, there appeared before us a man in extremely white clothes and with extremely black hair. No trace of journeying was visible on him, and none of us knew him. He sat close to the Prophet ﷺ, rested his knees against his knees and placed his hands on his thighs, and said, "O Muhammad! Tell me about Islām." The Messenger of Allāh ﷺ said, "Islām is that you should testify that there is no god except Allāh and that Muhammad is His Messenger, that you should establish salāh, pay zakāh, fast during (the month of) Ramadhān, and perform hajj to the House if you are able to do so." The man remarked, "You have spoken truly." We were astonished that he is questioning him and also confirming his answer to be correct.

Then he said, "Tell me about Īmān." The Messenger ﷺ replied, "Īmān is that you believe in Allāh, His angels, His Books, His Messengers, the Last Day, and in Qadar (fate), the good of it and the evil of it." The man remarked, "You have spoken truly."

Then he said, "Tell me about Ihsān." The Messenger ﷺ answered, "Ihsān is that you should serve Allāh as though you could see Him, for though you cannot see Him yet (know that) He sees you."

Then the man said, "Tell me about the Hour." The Messenger ﷺ said, "The one being questioned about it knows no more than the questioner." So he said, "Then tell me about its signs." The Messenger ﷺ said, "They are that the slave-girl will give birth to her mistress; and that you will see the barefooted, naked, destitute, shepherds competing with one another in raising lofty buildings."

Thereupon the man left. I waited a while, and then the Messenger of Allāh ﷺ said, "O 'Umar, do you know who that questioner was?" I replied, "Allāh and His Messenger know best." He said, "That was Jibrīl. He came to teach you your religion." [Muslim]

This hadīth teaches us that there are four essential branches of religious studies (Islamic Theology) that all Muslims should undertake:

1. Beliefs (Islamic Creed)
2. Practice (Islamic Law)
3. Character & Behaviour (Islamic Spirituality)
4. The Final Hour (Islamic Eschatology)

The final part of this hadīth means that Sayyidunā Jibrīl عليه السلام came to teach the noble Companions رضي الله عنهم about their religion by asking the Messenger ﷺ some very simple yet important questions in their presence, so that they may benefit by listening to his answers.

THE SIX ARTICLES OF FAITH IN ISLĀM

Questions

1. What are the two sources of the religion of Islām?
2. Why is faith in the Messenger given primary importance in Islām?
3. How is Islām a complete way of life?
4. What are the two things that one must do to become a Muslim?
5. What is the meaning of tawhīd?
6. What is the meaning of kufr?
7. What is the meaning of shirk?
8. Why do you think kufr and shirk are unforgivable sins?
9. Give an example of shirk in Allāh's ﷻ attributes.
10. What are the five pillars of Islām?
11. Why is the shahādah the most important pillar of Islām?
12. What are the six articles of creed in Islām?
13. What is the meaning of salvation?
14. What are the five benefits of faith?
15. What questions did Angel Jibrīl عليه السلام ask the Prophet ﷺ?
16. What are the four essential branches of Islamic Studies?

Chapter 1

Belief in Allāh سُبْحَانَهُ وَتَعَالَىٰ

Belief in Allāh سبحانه وتعالى

1. Allāh سبحانه وتعالى exists. His existence is the greatest and the most obvious truth. He is as He has described Himself.
2. Allāh سبحانه وتعالى is Preeternal: He has always existed, without a beginning.
3. Allāh سبحانه وتعالى is Eternal and Ever-Living: He will always exist, without an end. He does not perish or die.
4. Allāh سبحانه وتعالى is Absolute: He exists independently. He is not dependant or in need of anything. He does not require any support or care. His creation can neither benefit, harm, or influence Him in any way.
5. Allāh سبحانه وتعالى is Transcendent: He exists beyond the material universe. He is not subject to the laws of His creation and the limitations of time, space and matter.
6. Allāh سبحانه وتعالى is Perpetual: He exists without any change, growth or decline in His essence or attributes.
7. Allāh سبحانه وتعالى is One: He has no parent, spouse, child, equal, partner or rival.
8. Allāh سبحانه وتعالى is Infinite: He cannot be measured, calculated, restricted or comprehended.
9. Allāh سبحانه وتعالى is Unique: He has no resemblance. There can be nothing like Him in essence or attribute.
10. Allāh سبحانه وتعالى is Perfect and Flawless. He is free from all faults and deficiencies.
11. Allāh سبحانه وتعالى is the Creator. He alone can create from nothing.

12. Allāh ﷻ is the sole Owner of the universe.
13. Allāh ﷻ has full authority and control over His creation. Everything occurs as He orders and specifies. His decree cannot be prevented or hindered and His judgement cannot be overruled.
14. Allāh ﷻ is the Sustainer. He looks after and provides for the entire universe. Everything is in need of His care.
15. Allāh ﷻ does as He wills. He is not questioned about what He does. He does not require anyone's advice. He is not under anyone's orders or instructions.
16. Allāh ﷻ is Omnipotent: He has limitless power and ability.
17. Allāh ﷻ is Invincible: nothing can intimidate Him, threaten Him, overpower Him, or make Him vulnerable.
18. Allāh ﷻ is Omniscient: He has absolute knowledge of everything. Nothing is hidden from Him.
19. Allāh ﷻ is the All-Hearing.
20. Allāh ﷻ is the All-Seeing.
21. Allāh ﷻ is Divine and Holy. He has the best attributes. He is the source of all good. He is the only being truly worthy of worship.
22. Allāh ﷻ communicates with His creation via speech and inspiration. His speech is His divine attribute and unlike the speech of created things.

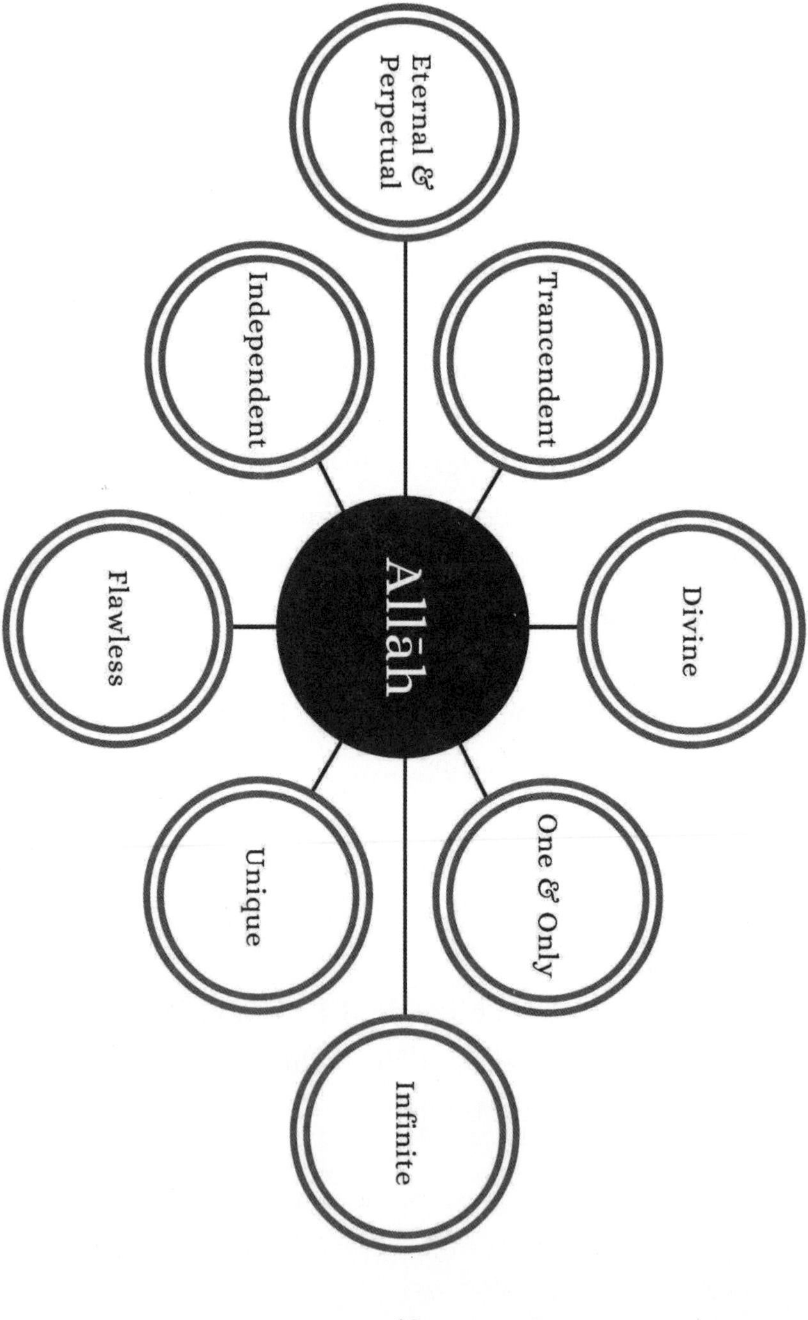
Allāh
Eternal & Perpetual
Trancendent
Divine
One & Only
Infinite
Unique
Flawless
Independent

The Blessed Names of Allāh ﷻ

Allāh ﷻ says in the glorious Qur'ān:

﴿ اللَّهُ لَا إِلَٰهَ إِلَّا هُوَ لَهُ الْأَسْمَاءُ الْحُسْنَىٰ ﴾

"Allāh, there is no god but He. For Him are the best names." (20: 8)

By reflecting over the meanings of these names we can better understand our Creator. We can also begin to appreciate how He is relevant to us in all aspects of our life and make sense of our life experiences.

Muslims are required to do the following with regard to the blessed names of Allāh ﷻ:

1. To believe in Allāh ﷻ with His names and qualities He has attributed to Himself.
2. To understand and reflect over the meanings of these blessed names.
3. To accept the implications of these blessed names.
4. To call upon Allāh ﷻ using these blessed names.
5. To praise and glorify Allāh ﷻ with these blessed names.
6. To adopt those qualities that are possible and permissible for us to follow such as kindness and patience.
7. To refrain from adopting or imitating those qualities that are not permissible for us to adopt, such as legislation i.e. making our own rules and regulations up in religion.

1. اَلرَّحْمٰنُ

Ar-Rahmān

The Most Beneficent

2. اَلرَّحِيْمُ

Ar-Rahīm

The Most Merciful

3. اَلْاَحَدُ

Al-Ahad

The Only

4. اَلصَّمَدُ

As-Samad

The Independent

5. اَلسَّمِيْعُ

As-Samī'

The All-Hearing

6. اَلْبَصِيْرُ

Al-Basīr

The All-Seeing

7. اَلْوَاسِعُ

Al-Wāsi'

The Infinite

8. اَلْعَلِيْمُ

Al-'Alīm

The All-Knowing

9. اَلْخَالِقُ

Al-Khāliq

The Creator

10. اَلْفَاطِرُ

Al-Fātir

The Inventor

11. اَلْأَوَّلُ

Al-Awwal

The First

12. اَلْآخِرُ

Al-Ākhir

The Last

13. اَلظَّاهِرُ

Az-Zāhir

The Manifest

14. اَلْبَاطِنُ

Al-Bātin

The Hidden

15. اَلْحَيُّ

Al-Hayy

The Living

16. اَلْقَيُّومُ

Al-Qayyūm

The Maintainer

17. اَلْغَنِيُّ
Al-Ghaniyy
The Self-Sufficient

18. اَلْحَمِيْدُ
Al-Hamīd
The Praiseworthy

19. اَلْعَلِيُّ
Al-'Aliyy
The High

20. اَلْعَظِيْمُ
Al-'Azīm
The Magnificent

21. اَلْغَفُوْرُ
Al-Ghafūr
The All-Forgiving

22. اَلْوَدُوْدُ
Al-Wadūd
The Loving

23. اَلشَّكُوْرُ
Ash-Shakūr
The Most Appreciative

24. اَلْحَلِيْمُ
Al-Halīm
The Clement

25. اَلْحَقُّ
Al-Haqq
The Truth

26. اَلْمُبِيْنُ
Al-Mubīn
The Clear

27. اَلْعَزِيْزُ
Al-Azīz
The Almighty

28. اَلْحَكِيْمُ
Al-Hakīm
The Wise

29. اَلْوَلِيُّ
Al-Waliyy
The Guardian

30. اَلنَّصِيْرُ
An-Nasīr
The Helper

31. اَللَّطِيْفُ
Al-Latīf
The Subtle

32. اَلْخَبِيْرُ
Al-Khabīr
The All-Aware

33. اَلْقَرِيْبُ
Al-Qarīb
The Close

34. اَلْمُجِيْبُ
Al-Mujīb
The Responsive

35. اَلرَّزَّاقُ
Ar-Razzāq
The Provider

36. اَلْمَتِيْنُ
Al-Matīn
The Firm

37. اَلْوَاحِدُ
Al-Wāhid
The One

38. اَلْقَهَّارُ
Al-Qahhār
The Dominant

39. اَلْوَهَّابُ
Al-Wahhāb
The Bountiful

40. اَلتَّوَّابُ
At-Tawwāb
The Pardoner

Questions

1. What do the following statements mean?
    i. Allāh ﷾ is Absolute.
    ii. Allāh ﷾ is Transcendent.
    iii. Allāh ﷾ is Perpetual.
    iv. Allāh ﷾ is Infinite.
    v. Allāh ﷾ is Omnipotent.
    vi. Allāh ﷾ is Omniscient.
    vii. Allāh ﷾ is Unique.
    viii. Allāh ﷾ is Preeternal.
    ix. Allāh ﷾ is Eternal.
2. What is unique about Allāh's ﷾ attribute of creation?
3. How should a believer act after knowing and believing that Allāh ﷾ is ar-Razzāq (the Provider)?
4. How can learning the beautiful names of Allāh ﷾ help a believer in his journey through life? Explain your answer with an example.
5. What are the seven rights that Muslims are required to fulfil with regard to the blessed names of Allāh ﷾?
6. Why is the denial of Allāh's ﷾ existence the greatest sin?
7. Why can there be no other god besides Allāh ﷾, the one and only God?
8. State ten names of Allāh ﷾?

ذَٰلِكُمُ اللَّهُ رَبُّكُمْ لَا إِلَٰهَ إِلَّا هُوَ خَالِقُ كُلِّ شَيْءٍ فَاعْبُدُوهُ وَهُوَ عَلَىٰ
كُلِّ شَيْءٍ وَكِيلٌ ۝

"That is Allāh, your Lord. There is no god but He, the Creator of everything. So worship Him. He is Guardian over everything." (6:102)

Chapter 2
Belief in Allāh's ﷻ Angels

Belief in Allah's ﷻ Angels

1. Angels are the slaves of Allāh ﷻ.
2. Angels are created from nūr (a special light).
3. Angels are immortal beings: they do not die.
4. Angels live in the unseen world.
5. Angels are extremely powerful and have great abilities.
6. Angels do not get tired or exhausted.
7. Angels have the ability to take on human form.
8. Angels are free from human needs like food and sleep.
9. Angels have no gender: they are neither male nor female.
10. Angels do not disobey Allāh ﷻ or act against His will.
11. Angels are punctual and reliable. They get the work done.
12. Angels are free from evil traits such as pride, greed, hate and jealousy.
13. Only Allāh ﷻ knows the number of angels in existence.
14. Allāh ﷻ has given angels different roles and duties.
15. There are four well-known archangels:
    (a) Jibrīl عليه السلام: The angel of revelation.
    (b) Mīkā'īl عليه السلام: The angel of weather and sustenance.
    (c) Isrāfīl عليه السلام: The angel of the trumpet.
    (d) Izrā'īl (Malak al-Mawt) عليه السلام: The angel of death.

14. There are also some well known group-angels:
    a) Kirāman Kātibīn: The noble scribes who record every action of human beings.
    b) Munkar and Nakīr: The questioners in the grave.

THE ARCHANGELS

Jibrīl

The angel of revelation & punishment

Mīkā'īl

The angel of weather & sustenance

Izrā'īl

The angel of death who takes souls

Isrāfīl

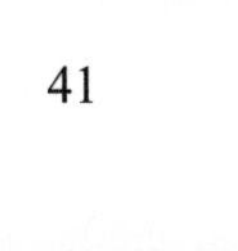

The angel of destruction and revival.

Archangels

Jibrīl عليه السلام: The angel of revelation

1. Jibrīl عليه السلام is the chief messenger angel. Allāh سبحانه وتعالى sent His books and commands to the Messengers through him.
2. He also brought down Allāh's سبحانه وتعالى punishments upon those who earned His wrath.
3. He is highly trustworthy , reliable and mighty.

Mīkā'īl عليه السلام: The angel of weather and sustenance

1. Mīkā'īl عليه السلام is the chief angel of the weather and food.
2. Many angels work under his supervision in controlling the wind, moving the clouds, providing rain, producing vegetation and sustaining life on earth.

Isrāfīl عليه السلام: The angel of the trumpet

1. Isrāfīl's عليه السلام duty is to blow the trumpet and destroy the universe at the command of Allāh سبحانه وتعالى at its ordained time.
2. Ever since he was given the task, his eyes have been fixed on the Throne of Allāh سبحانه وتعالى.

Izrā'īl عليه السلام: The angel of death

1. Izrā'īl عليه السلام, also known as Malak al-Mawt, is in charge of taking away souls at their appointed times.
2. A team of angels work under him: some take away the lives of pious people with care, while others take away the lives of sinners and disbelievers with aggression and force.

Group Angels

The recording angels

1. Every person has an angel to his right and an angel to his left who are appointed by Allāh ﷻ as guardians over us.
2. These angels are known by the following group names:
   - ⇒ Hafazah (the Guardians)
   - ⇒ Kirāman Kātibīn (the Noble Scribes)
3. They record every behaviour of consequence, be it our actions or utterances.
4. They are highly accurate and always prepared. They never make a mistake or miss anything out.
5. The angel on the right records all the good behaviour.
6. The angel on the left records all the bad behaviour.
7. The scribes work in shifts that change twice a day: at the time of Fajr prayer and at the time of 'Asr prayer. At the end of every shift, a new pair of angels descend while the current scribes return to the heavens with our records. Allāh ﷻ asks the returning angels about the condition they left us in, though He knows better.
8. Our records will be used on the Day of Judgement to decide our ultimate fate and final destination.
9. Allāh ﷻ promises to reward good behaviour and warns that He will punish bad behaviour.
10. Being aware of these angels will help us become more conscious of Allāh ﷻ and live lives of virtue and purpose.

Good and bad deeds

1. A good deed is any action that Allāh ﷻ or His Messenger ﷺ have commanded or encouraged us to do, and which the Sharī'ah considers to be virtuous and rewardable.
2. A bad deed is any action that Allāh ﷻ or His Messenger ﷺ have prohibited and discouraged us from doing, and which the Sharī'ah considers to be sinful and punishable.
3. Not all deeds are of the same value. Some good deeds are more virtuous and rewarding in comparison to other good deeds. Similarly, some bad deeds are more evil and punishable compared to other bad deeds.
4. We must make every effort to refrain from all major bad deeds (kabā'ir) at any cost, and fulfil all major good deeds to the best of our ability. We must also strive to stay away from minor bad deeds (saghā'ir), and aim to practice as many minor good deeds as we can.
5. Good deeds will come to a person's grave in pleasant forms, and will provide peace and security to the doer of the deed.
6. Bad deeds will come in ugly, terrifying appearances and forms, and will inflict the doer of the deed with painful punishment.
7. Good deeds will be the only valuable asset a person will have in the next world.
8. No amount of money or property will benefit a person in the Hereafter against the consequences of his bad deeds.

9. Good deeds are accepted and rewarded if they meet two conditions:
    i. They are done with sincerity i.e. with the intention of obeying Allāh ﷻ, fulfilling His command and gaining His pleasure.
    ii. They are done in accordance with the way shown and approved by the Prophet ﷺ i.e. it is in line with the established Prophetic Sunnah.
10. To take the laws of Allāh ﷻ lightly, by neglecting His laws and not taking His warnings or disobedience seriously is highly offensive and sinful, and may lead one to disbelief.

Heresy and Blasphemy

a) To regard established sins as lawful is heresy.
    i. Heresy: Deviation and departure from the fold of Islām by holding a belief or view that contradicts an established belief or law of Islām by way of unacceptable interpretation.

b) To insult or make fun of any established belief, command or teaching of Islām is blasphemy.
    ii. Blasphemy: Deviation and departure from the fold of Islām by way of disrespecting and violating the sanctity of an established belief or law of Islām and that which is sacred in the Religion.

The Testers of the Grave

1. When a person dies, he will be met by two angels called Munkar and Nakīr, who will question him. This is known as the fitnah (trial) of the grave. Their eyes are like dazzling lightning and their voices like deafening thunder. They come with a whip so heavy that if the whole world were to try and lift it together, they would not be able to.
2. They will only question the deceased about his faith. They will make him sit up and ask him three questions:
    - ⇒ Who is your Lord?
    - ⇒ What is your religion?
    - ⇒ What did you believe about the man sent to you?
3. A person's ability to answer these questions will depend on the quality of his faith and submission to Allāh ﷻ.
4. If he gives the right answers, he will be shown his place in Jannah and the place Allāh ﷻ saved him from in Jahannam. His grave will be widened and he will rest in peace.
5. If he cannot answer the questions, he will receive a severe lashing. He will be struck with an iron hammer between his ears, and his cry will be heard by whatever approaches him except human beings and jinns. The earth will be told to squeeze him until his ribs are interlocked. He will remain crushed until Allāh ﷻ raises him.
6. Allāh ﷻ will grant strength to those who believe in the firmly rooted word (kalimat al-Islām) so that they can withstand the trials of this world and the Hereafter.

Questions

1. What is an angel made of?
2. Are angels male or female?
3. How many angels are there?
4. What do angels do?
5. What qualities do angels have that make them so reliable?
6. What are some of the key differences between angels and humans?
7. Name the four archangels and their duties.
8. What are the angels who record our deeds known as?
9. What is a good deed?
10. What is a bad deed?
11. When is a good deed acceptable in the sight of Allāh ﷻ?
12. What are the angels (testers) of the grave known as? Describe them.
13. What are the three questions a person will be asked by the angels in the grave?
14. How will a person be able to pass the test of the grave?
15. How can belief in angels help us become better people and more conscious of Allāh ﷻ?

يُنَزِّلُ الْمَلٰٓئِكَةَ بِالرُّوْحِ مِنْ اَمْرِهٖ عَلٰى مَنْ يَّشَآءُ مِنْ عِبَادِهٖٓ اَنْ
اَنْذِرُوْٓا اَنَّهٗ لَآ اِلٰهَ اِلَّآ اَنَا فَاتَّقُوْنِ ۝

"(It is) He (Allāh Who) sends down the Angel (Jibrīl) with the Spirit (of life, that is the Revelation), (who descends) by His command upon whomsoever He wills from amongst His servants (with the message to) 'warn the people that there is none worthy of worship expect Me, so be mindful of Me.'" (16:2)

Chapter 3

Belief in Allāh's سُبْحَانَهُ وَتَعَالَىٰ Books

Belief in Allāh's ﷻ Books

1. Allāh ﷻ sent guidance to mankind through Messengers, who received His revelation in three ways:
   - ⇒ Divine inspiration directly to the heart.
   - ⇒ Communication behind a veil.
   - ⇒ Revelation via a messenger angel.
2. Allāh ﷻ revealed scriptures to some of His Messengers, which contained guidance for mankind in relation to their beliefs, conduct and character.
3. There are four major scriptures that were revealed:
   - ⇒ Tawrāh - revealed to Mūsā عليه السلام.
   - ⇒ Zabūr - revealed to Dāwūd عليه السلام.
   - ⇒ Injīl - revealed to 'Īsā عليه السلام.
   - ⇒ Qur'ān - revealed to Muhammad ﷺ.
4. The primary message in all scriptures has always been the same: there is no god but Allāh ﷻ and everyone shall return to Him after death.
5. Besides the glorious Qur'ān, all other scriptures have been corrupted and are no longer in their original form.
6. It is necessary to believe in the truthfulness of all the divine scriptures as they were in their original form.
7. All scriptures were authoritative (accurate) in their respective times.
8. The glorious Qur'ān replaced all previous scriptures in authority and sacred law. It will remain the only authoritative scripture until the Day of Judgement.

SCRIPTURES

TAWRĀH

The Old Testament

Received by:
Prophet Mūsā عليه السلام
(peace be upon him)

ZABŪR

The Psalms

Received by:
Prophet Dāwūd عليه السلام
(peace be upon him)

INJĪL

The New Testament

Received by:
Prophet 'Īsā عليه السلام
(peace be upon him)

QUR'ĀN

The Final Testament

Received by:
Prophet Muhammad ﷺ
(peace be upon him)

The Glorious Qur'ān

1. The glorious Qur'ān is the final book of Allāh ﷻ. No other book will be revealed after it.
2. It was revealed to Muhammad ﷺ.
3. It is the greatest and most unique miracle of all.
4. It is the inimitable unique Arabic speech of Allāh ﷻ. His speech does not resemble His creation's speech in any way, and neither can it be matched.
5. It has a total of 114 sūrahs (chapters), beginning with sūrah al-Fātihah and ending with sūrah an-Nās.
6. It is the only scripture that remains in its original form and will remain so until the Last Day, as Allāh ﷻ has promised to protect it from corruption, both in word and meaning.
7. We believe in what it confirms as true; we reject what it rejects; and we suspend judgement and remain silent about anything it is silent about.
8. It is a timeless and universal book of guidance: It will continue to be relevant to every group, nation and society, and applicable in every time, place and situation.
9. It is the last sacred law (sharīʻah), which mankind must accept and abide by. It guides mankind towards the correct beliefs, actions, morals and values.
10. It supersedes and overrides all previous laws that were prescribed in previous scriptures.
11. To deny any part of the glorious Qur'ān is disbelief.

12. To hold a belief or view that is contrary to an established belief or law of the glorious Qur'ān is heresy.
    - Heresy: Deviation and departure from the fold of Islām by holding a belief or view that contradicts an established belief or law of Islām by way of unacceptable interpretation.
13. To insult or make fun of the glorious Qur'ān, or any established belief, command or teaching of the glorious Qur'ān is blasphemy.
    - Blasphemy: Deviation and departure from the fold of Islām by way of disrespecting and violating the sanctity of an established belief or law of Islām and that which is sacred in the Religion.

Names of the Glorious Qur'ān

The glorious Qur'ān has four primary names:

1.	Al-Kitāb	The Book/The Law
2.	Al-Qur'ān	The Recited Scripture
3.	Al-Furqān:	The Criterion
4.	Al-Dhikr:	The Reminder

Attributes of the Glorious Qur'ān

The following are some of the attributes of the glorious Qur'ān.

1.	Al-'Azīz	The Majestic, Magnificent
2.	Al-Majīd	The Glorious, The Excellent
3.	Al-Karīm	The Noble, The Generous
4.	Al-Mīzān	The Balance
5.	Al-Nūr	The Illuminator
6.	Al-'Adhīm:	The Sublime, The Majestic
7.	Al-Muhaymin	The Guardian, The Authentic

Rights of the Glorious Qur'ān:

Muslims must fulfil the following rights of the glorious Qur'ān:

1. To believe in its truth and accept its authority.
2. To recite it and listen to its recitation.
3. To study it and reflect over its meanings.
4. To act upon its laws and advice.
5. To teach and preach it.
6. To love and honour it.

Questions

1. Why did Allāh ﷻ reveal books to mankind?
2. What are the names of the four famous Books and the Prophets who received them?
3. What has been the primary message in all of the divine scriptures?
4. What has happened to all previous scriptures before the glorious Qur'ān?
5. How is the glorious Qur'ān different to other scriptures?
6. How many chapters does the glorious Qur'ān have?
7. What is the first sūrah of the glorious Qur'ān called?
8. What are the four primary names of the glorious Qur'ān and what do you learn from them?
9. State three attributes of the glorious Qur'ān and what you can learn from them.
10. What are the rights of the glorious Qur'ān that we must fulfil?
11. How do Muslims use the glorious Qur'ān to deal with the teachings found in the previous heavenly books?

وَهَٰذَا كِتَٰبٌ أَنزَلْنَٰهُ مُبَارَكٌ فَاتَّبِعُوهُ وَاتَّقُوا لَعَلَّكُمْ تُرْحَمُونَ ۝

"And this (the glorious Qur'ān) is a blessed Book that We have revealed. So follow it and be mindful (of Allāh) so that you may be shown mercy.'" (6:155)

Chapter 4
Belief in Allāh's ﷻ Messengers

Belief in Allāh's ﷻ Messengers

1. Messengers are of two types:
    (1) A rasūl is a messenger who receives a new law.
    (2) A nabī is a messenger who follows the law established by the previous rasūl.
2. From time to time, Allāh ﷻ sent Messengers to this world to guide people to the straight path, establish the truth of Islām, and serve as warners before the Day of Judgement.
3. They were chosen by Allāh ﷻ to represent Islām and be the link between Him and His subjects.
4. They were men of piety, nobility and great character. They were truthful, caring, selfless and intelligent.
5. All Messengers of Allāh ﷻ preached the same message: there is no god besides Allāh ﷻ and we will all return to Him and be held accountable for our actions.
6. The Messengers are the most knowledgeable people of their nations in relation to the book of Allāh ﷻ.
7. Allāh ﷻ gave authority to the Messengers and commanded the people to obey them.
8. There is no position higher than the position of nubuwwah and risālah (the two levels of prophethood).
9. The Messengers of Allāh ﷻ were under divine protection from the influence of Shaytān and from committing sins.
10. To reject any of the Messengers is disbelief, and to insult, dismiss or disregard them is heresy.

Names of the Messengers

There are twenty five Messengers (Ambiyā and Rusul) mentioned in the glorious Qur'ān by name. They are as follows:

1. Sayyidunā Ādam عليه السلام
2. Sayyidunā Idrīs عليه السلام
3. Sayyidunā Nūh عليه السلام
4. Sayyidunā Hūd عليه السلام
5. Sayyidunā Sālih عليه السلام
6. Sayyidunā Lūt عليه السلام
7. Sayyidunā Ibrāhīm عليه السلام
8. Sayyidunā Ismā'īl عليه السلام
9. Sayyidunā Ishāq عليه السلام
10. Sayyidunā Ya'qūb عليه السلام
11. Sayyidunā Yūsuf عليه السلام
12. Sayyidunā Shu'ayb عليه السلام
13. Sayyidunā Mūsā عليه السلام
14. Sayyidunā Hārūn عليه السلام
15. Sayyidunā Dāwūd عليه السلام
16. Sayyidunā Sulaymān عليه السلام
17. Sayyidunā Ayyūb عليه السلام
18. Sayyidunā Dhul Kifl عليه السلام
19. Sayyidunā Yūnus عليه السلام
20. Sayyidunā Ilyās عليه السلام
21. Sayyidunā Al-Yasa' عليه السلام
22. Sayyidunā Zakariyyā عليه السلام
23. Sayyidunā Yahyā عليه السلام
24. Sayyidunā 'Īsā عليه السلام

25. Sayyidunā Muhammad ﷺ

Prophet Muhammad ﷺ

1. Muhammad ﷺ was the last and final Messenger of Allāh تعالى and the seal of prophethood: no messenger (nabī or rasūl) will come after him.
2. He is the leader of all Messengers and the best of creation.
3. It was his duty to convey the Revelation, teach mankind its meaning and the application of its laws, and purify them. The holy Prophet ﷺ fulfilled his duty in the most complete and excellent manner.
4. Allāh تعالى revealed the glorious Qur'ān to him via the angel Jibrīl عليه السلام, enabled him to preserve it in his blessed heart, and also taught him its explanation.
5. There is nobody more knowledgable of the book of Allāh تعالى than the holy Prophet ﷺ. He was also given much knowledge of the unseen. His knowledge is unparalleled.
6. He is a timeless model for mankind.
7. He established a religious model called the Sunnah or the Hikmah. This is the last and best Sharī'ah (Sacred Law).
8. Allāh تعالى has made it obligatory upon Muslims to love and respect His Messenger; accept and abide by his teachings (Sunnah); and follow his beautiful example (Uswah).
9. To deny or refuse to accept the Sharī'ah that is based on the Qur'an and established Sunnah is disbelief.
10. It is necessary to respect and honour the holy Prophet's ﷺ household, his family and his Companions رضي الله عنهم.

THE ROLE OF
THE MESSENGER

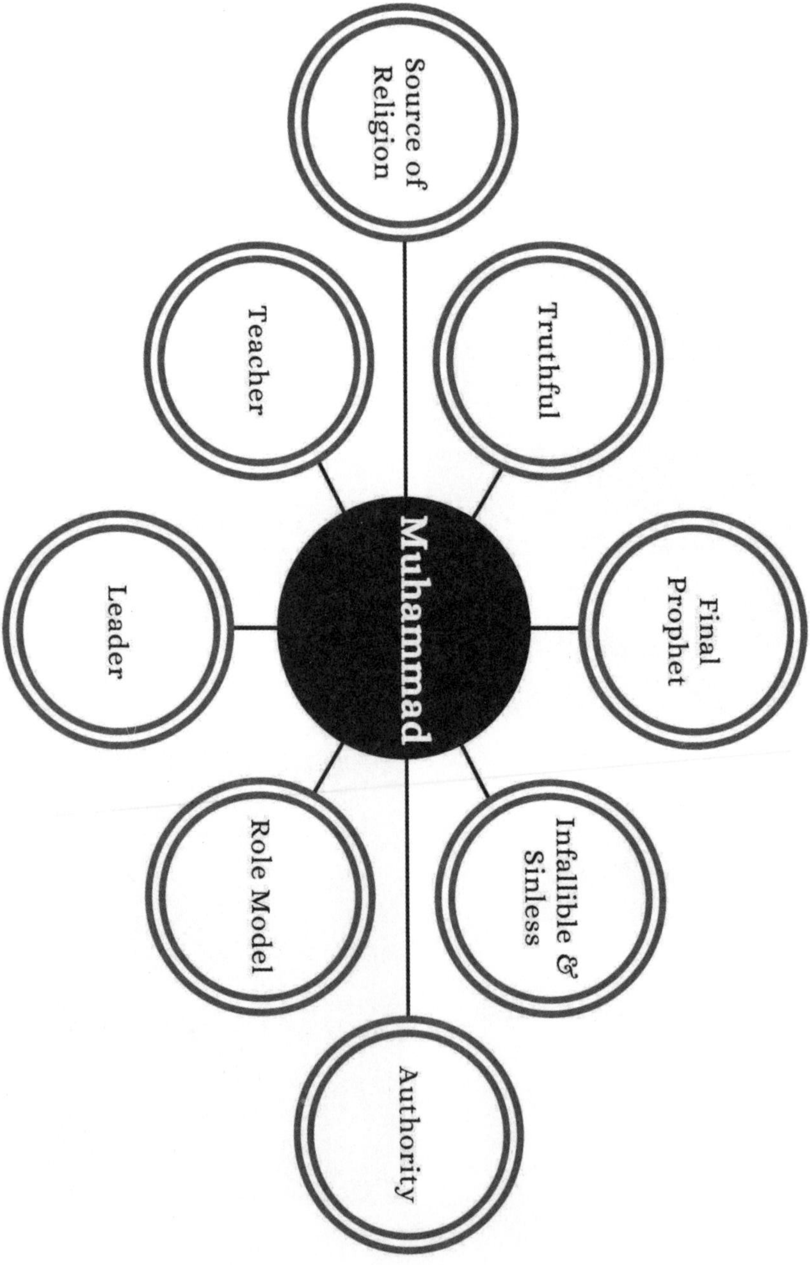
Muhammad
Source of Religion
Truthful
Final Prophet
Infallible & Sinless
Authority
Role Model
Leader
Teacher

The Ten Companions Promised Jannah

1. Abū Bakr ibn Abī Quhāfah رضي الله عنه.
2. 'Umar ibn al-Khattāb رضي الله عنه.
3. 'Uthmān ibn 'Affān رضي الله عنه.
4. 'Ali ibn Abī Tālib رضي الله عنه.
5. Talhah ibn 'Ubaydillāh رضي الله عنه.
6. Zubair ibn al-'Awwām رضي الله عنه.
7. 'Abdur Rahmān ibn 'Awf رضي الله عنه.
8. Sa'd ibn Abī Waqqās رضي الله عنه.
9. Sa'īd ibn Zayd رضي الله عنه.
10. Abū 'Ubaydah ibn al-Jarrāh رضي الله عنه.

Other Notable Companions

1. 'Abdullāh ibn Mas'ūd رضي الله عنه.
2. 'Abdullāh ibn 'Abbās رضي الله عنه.
3. 'Abdullāh ibn 'Umar رضي الله عنه.
4. Anas ibn Mālik رضي الله عنه
5. Mu'ādh ibn Jabal رضي الله عنه.
6. Bilāl ibn Rabāh رضي الله عنه.
7. Khālid ibn al-Walīd رضي الله عنه.
8. Abū Hurairah رضي الله عنه.
9. Mu'āwiyah ibn Abī Sufyān رضي الله عنه.
10. Salmān al-Fārsī رضي الله عنه.

The Family of Prophet Muhammad ﷺ

Wives

1. Khadījah bint Khuwailid ﵂.
2. Sawdah bint Zam'ah ﵂.
3. 'Āishah bint Abī Bakr ﵂.
4. Hafsah bint Umar ﵂.
5. Zaynab bint Khuzaymah ﵂.
6. Hind bint Suhail (Ummu Salamah) ﵂.
7. Zaynab bint Jahsh ﵂.
8. Juwayriyyah bint al-Hārith ﵂.
9. Safiyyah bint Huyay ﵂.
10. Ramlah bint Abī Sufyān (Ummu Habībah) ﵂.
11. Maymūnah bint al-Hārith ﵂.

Children

1. Qāsim ﵁.
2. 'Abdullāh (Tāhir/Tayyib) ﵁.
3. Zaynab ﵂.
4. Ruqayyah ﵂.
5. Ummu Kulthūm ﵂.
6. Fātimah ﵂.
7. Ibrāhīm ﵁.

All of the holy Prophet's ﷺ children were born to his first wife, Sayyidah Khadījah ﵂, except for Ibrāhīm, who was born to Māriyah Qibtiyyah.

Miracles

1. A miracle is an extraordinary act that goes against the laws of science and nature. In other words, it is an act that is scientifically impossible and logically unbelievable.
2. A miracle is not magic, sorcery or trickery.
3. The Messengers of Allāh سبحانه وتعالى sometimes performed miracles to prove the truth of their claim to prophethood.
4. Miracles occurred with Allāh's سبحانه وتعالى will and in His name.
5. If a nation asked its Messenger for a miracle and was given one, and thereafter they rejected the Messenger, then they would be faced with the wrath of Allāh سبحانه وتعالى.

Examples of some miracles are:

1. The fire becoming cool for Prophet Ibrāhīm عليه السلام.
2. The staff of Prophet Mūsā عليه السلام becoming a snake and splitting the red sea with it.
3. Iron being made soft for Prophet Dāwūd عليه السلام.
4. Prophet Sulaymān عليه السلام being able to control the winds, the jinn and the animals.
5. Prophet 'Īsā عليه السلام being able to cure the leper, restore the vision of the blind, and bring the dead back to life.
6. Prophet Muhammad ﷺ travelling to al-Masjid al-Aqsā in Jerusalem, Palestine (may it be liberated and sanctified) - one of Islām's holy sites, its first Qiblah, and the second masjid on Earth and from there to the heavens, in the journeys known as al-Isrā and al-Mi'rāj respectively.

Intercession

On the Day of Judgement, everyone will face trial alone. There will be no relative, friend, lawyer, solicitor, or interpreter to help you. However, the holy Prophet ﷺ will be given special permission to intercede. This is known as the praised platform, or al-Maqām al-Mahmūd.

Intercession is the act of getting involved in another person's case in order to benefit him in some way.

The intercession of the holy Prophet ﷺ will be of ten types:

1. To get the Judgement started.
2. To get certain righteous believers into Jannah without reckoning.
3. To save sinful believers who have been sentenced to Hell from entering Hell by getting them pardoned.
4. To free sinful believers from Hell.
5. To reduce the punishment of other sinful believers who are sent to Hell and could not be pardoned and freed.
6. To get such people into Jannah whose good deeds and bad deeds are equal on the Scales.
7. To increase the reward/status of the successful believers.
8. To open up the gates of Jannah.
9. For the people of the blessed city of Madīnah.
10. For those who visited his grave.

Questions

1. Why does Allāh ﷻ send Messengers to people?
2. Name a few famous Messengers.
3. What is the role of the Messenger?
4. Why is it important to follow the Messenger's teachings and example?
5. What are some of the essential qualities of a Messenger?
6. How does one become a messenger?
7. Will there be any more Messengers to come after the Prophet Muhammad ﷺ? Why not?
8. What is a miracle?
9. Why did Messengers perform miracles?
10. Give examples of some famous miracles.
11. What are the names of the ten Companions ؓ who were promised Paradise?
12. What are the names of the Prophet's ﷺ wives?
13. What are the names of the Prophet's ﷺ children?
14. What are the names of some other Companions ؓ? Do you know what they are famously known for?
15. What is the meaning of shafā'ah and what are the ten ways in which it will be used on the Day of Judgement to benefit people?

وَمَنْ يُّطِعِ اللّٰهَ وَرَسُوْلَهٗ وَيَخْشَ اللّٰهَ وَيَتَّقْهِ فَاُولٰٓئِكَ هُمُ
الْفَآئِزُوْنَ ۞

"For whoever obeys Allāh and His Messenger, and fears Allāh and is mindful of Him, then such people are the victorious." (24:52)

Chapter 5
Belief in the Last Day

Belief in the Last Day

1. The Last Day refers to the beginning of the Afterlife i.e. the Day of Resurrection and beyond.
2. On the lead up to this day, the world will have no one left to glorify the blessed name of Allāh ﷻ. So Allāh ﷻ will instruct Isrāfīl ؑ to blow the sūr (trumpet), whose sound will cause the entire universe to perish. This is known as the Final Hour. It will occur suddenly, without any prior notice, upon the worst of people. The universe will be annihilated, and only Allāh ﷻ will remain.
3. When Allāh ﷻ wills, He will instruct Isrāfīl ؑ to blow the sūr once again, upon which the dead will be resurrected. This is known as al-ba'th ba'd al-mawt (the revival after death).
4. Mankind will be gathered for reckoning.
5. Every soul will appear in the court of Allāh ﷻ, alone. People will not even ask about their own family members. Instead, they will run away from them.
6. On that day, no soul will bear the burden of another's wrongdoings.
7. Man will meet his fate: The believer will be admitted into Jannah (Heaven) and the disbeliever will be admitted into Jahannam (Hell).
8. This will be the Last Day, which will never come to an end with the Will of Allāh ﷻ.

Names of the Last Day

Other names of the Last Day are as follows:

1. Al-Yawm al-Maw'ūd (the Promised Day).
2. Al-Yawm al-Haqq (the Established Day).
3. Yawm al-Waqt al-Ma'lūm (the Day of Appointed Time).
4. Yawm al-Ba'th (the Day of Resurrection).
5. Yawm al-Khurūj (the Day of Exit).
6. Yawm al-Qiyāmah (the Day of Order).
7. Yawm al-Hashr (the Day of Gathering).
8. Yawm al-Jam' (the Day of Congregation).
9. Al-Yawm al-Mash-hūd (the Witnessed Day).
10. Yawm al-Faza' al-Akbar (the Day of Great Terror).
11. Yawm al-'Ard (the Day of Presentation).
12. Yawm al-Hisāb (the Day of Reckoning).
13. Yawm al-Dīn (the Day of Recompense).
14. Yawm al-Fat-h (the Day of Judgement).
15. Yawm al-Fasl (the Day of Decree).
16. Yawm al-Hasrah (the Day of Regret).
17. Yawm al-Taghābun (the Day of Loss).
18. Yawm al-Wa'īd (the Day of (realising) the Warning).
19. Yawm al-Āzifah (the Day of Approaching Horror).
20. Yawm al-Tanād (the Day of Crying out).
21. Yawm al-Talāq (the Day of Meeting).
22. Yawm al-Khulūd (the Day of Eternity).

Signs of the Last Day

Only Allāh ﷻ knows exactly when the world will end. However, the holy Prophet ﷺ told us of some signs before its approach. Some of these signs are as follows:

1. Knowledge will be withdrawn and ignorance will prevail.
2. Immorality will become common.
3. Alcohol and drug abuse will rise.
4. Natural disasters will increase.
5. Time will lose its blessing.
6. People will not care about earning halāl (lawful) income.
7. Pious people will pass away without replacement.
8. Trust will be lifted.
9. Extreme greed will become widespread.
10. Ties of kinship will be severed.
11. Killing and injustice will rise.
12. Lies will dominate the world.
13. Ribā (interest) will engulf the world.
14. The religion of Islām will start to become strange.
15. Those practicing Islām will begin to face great difficulty.
16. Dajjāl, the Antichrist (False Messiah) will appear.
17. Prophet 'Īsā (Jesus Christ) عليه السلام, the Messiah will descend.
18. Ya'jūj and Ma'jūj will emerge.
19. The sun will rise from the west.
20. The Beast (Dābbah) will emerge with the ring of Prophet Sulaymān عليه السلام and the staff of Prophet Mūsā عليه السلام.

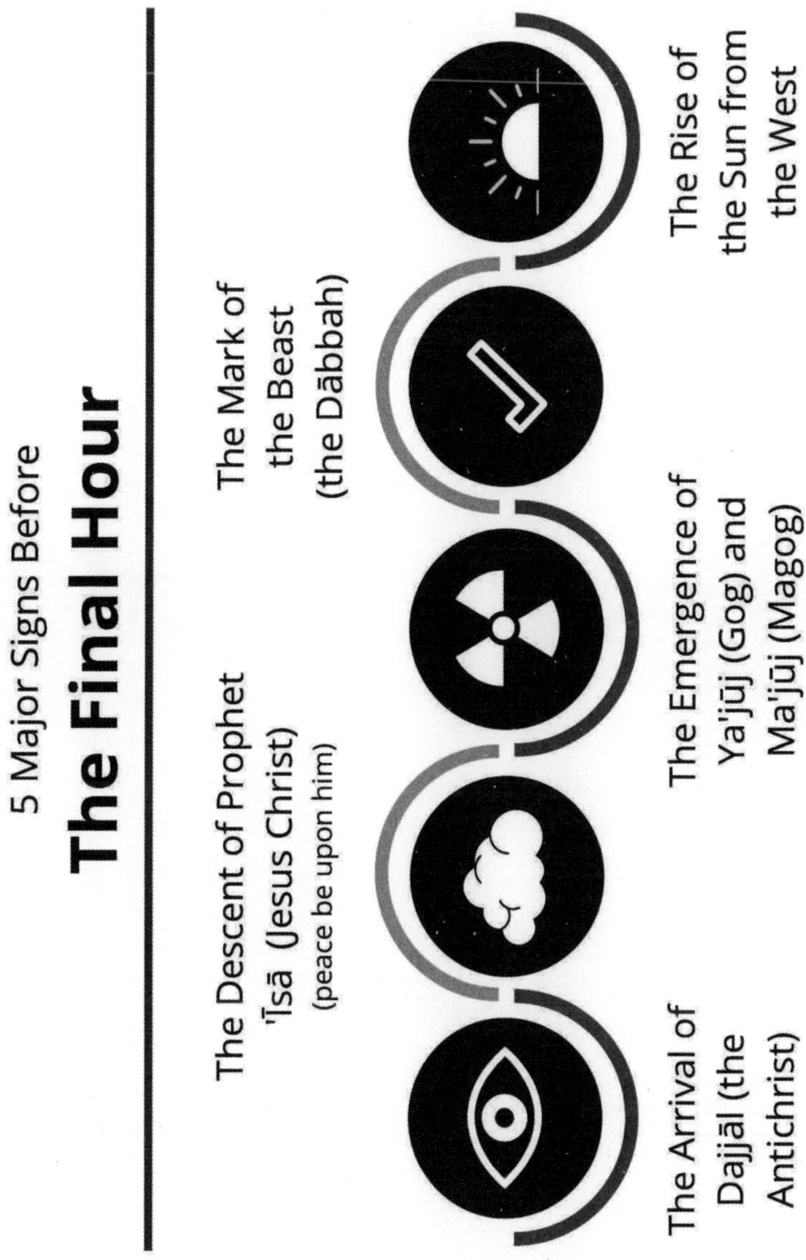
5 Major Signs Before
The Final Hour
The Arrival of Dajjāl (the Antichrist)
The Descent of Prophet 'Īsā (Jesus Christ) (peace be upon him)
The Emergence of Ya'jūj (Gog) and Ma'jūj (Magog)
The Mark of the Beast (the Dābbah)
The Rise of the Sun from the West

Barzakh

1. Barzakh is the first stage of the Afterlife.
2. It is a barrier between the physical and spiritual worlds, and the period between one's death and the Day of Judgement.
3. When a soul passes on, it is held in the Barzakh until the Day of Judgement, when everyone will be resurrected.
4. No soul can return to the world once it has passed on to the Barzakh.
5. In this period the good souls are left to rest in peace and the evil souls are punished.
6. The Barzakh is generally understood to exist in the grave, though it can exist anywhere and is not restricted to an actual grave.
7. The trial and punishment of the grave is true.
8. The grave is either a garden from the gardens of Heaven or a pit from the pits of Hell.
9. If a person succeeds in the grave then what follows will be easy. If one fails, then what follows will be more difficult.
10. When a person dies, his soul moves into the Barzakh and his book of records is sealed. He can thereafter only receive the benefit of three kinds of deeds:
    - ⇒ Beneficial knowledge that he left behind.
    - ⇒ Ongoing charity that he initiated.
    - ⇒ The prayer of another on his behalf.

Stages of the Last Day

Stage 1: The Revival and the Gathering

- After the world has been brought back into existence, Allāh ﷻ will send down rain, which will cause the dead to rise.
- All of mankind will be gathered onto one plain of land.
- The sun will be brought as close as a mile's distance. People will be drenched in their own sweat in ratio to their sins. Some will be up to their ankles, some up to their knees, some up to their waists, some up to their necks, some up to their mouths, and some will be totally submerged.
- People will seem intoxicated, but it will be the effect of Allāh's ﷻ punishment upon them.
- Everyone will be gathered unclothed until Allāh ﷻ clothes them, yet no one will notice anything due to the intense fear and distress they will be under.
- Nobody will be able to speak in the court of Allāh ﷻ on that day except with His permission.
- People will try to run away and hide from those who they know will have a case against them for some wrongdoing.
- Friends will become enemies of one another on this day, except for the people of piety.
- The wait will be intense. Eventually, the holy Prophet ﷺ will request for the Judgement proceedings to begin, and Allāh ﷻ will honour His request.

Stage 2: The Pond of al-Kawthar

- On the Day of Judgement, every prophet will have a pond from which his nation can drink.
- Our Prophet Muhammad ﷺ will have the largest pond, known as Hawd al-Kawthar.
- This pond will be an outlet of the great river in Jannah, known as al-Kawthar, that Allāh ﷻ gifted him. This river also supplies all other rivers in Jannah.
- The size of this pond is a month's distance of travel.
- It has gold and silver cups equivalent to the number of stars in the sky.
- Its taste is sweeter than honey, its colour is whiter than milk, and its fragrance is more pleasant than musk.
- Those who drink from the pond of al-Kawthar will never feel thirsty again.
- Before the judgement begins, people will flock to drink from this blessed pond and quench their thirst.
- The pond will be guarded by angels, and the Prophet ﷺ will be there to receive as many people as he can.
- The angels will only allow good people to drink from it, and drive bad people away from it.
- Amongst those who will be driven away from the pond are the hypocrites, extremely evil and immoral people, and those who introduced, practiced, and promoted unacceptable ways and ideas into Islām and strayed from the Sunnah in faith and practice.

Stage 3: The Judgement and the Scales

- Certain groups of believers will be given immediate entry into Jannah, without any accounting. They will be from the best of people. The Messengers of Allāh ﷾ and other pious servants of Allāh ﷾ will be exempt from reckoning. They will be protected from the difficulties of that day and granted shade under the Throne of Allāh ﷾.
- As for the disbelievers, some will be thrown straight into Hell without delay. Others will be told to follow the false gods they worshipped and thus will be lead to the fire.
- The remaining believers and hypocrites will be made to line up for reckoning. One by one they will be summoned to collect their records. These books will be accurate and will not have missed any deed out - good or bad, big or small, public or private.
- The pious will receive their books in the right hand. When they present themselves at the Scales for weighing, their scales will be heavy with virtues. Their good deeds will be rewarded and their bad deeds will be overlooked.
- The evil ones will be those who receive their books in the left hand. Their bad deeds will outweigh their good. When they present themselves at the Scales, their deeds will be scrutinised and they will be in trouble.
- The holy Prophet ﷺ will be allowed to intercede for his followers, as will the righteous believers, pious scholars and martyrs of his nation.

Stage 4: The Bridge

- Allāh ﷻ has created a bridge over Hell that is sharper than a sword, thinner than a strand of hair, slippery, dark and thorny.
- Every soul, good and bad, will cross this bridge, except for those wretched souls who will be sentenced to Hellfire before the judgement and weighing even begins.
- After the judgement, Allāh ﷻ will cover His nūr (light) so that there is utter darkness, and people will have to cross with the nūr (light) of their piety.
- The holy Prophet ﷺ and his nation (ummah) will be the first to cross the bridge, followed by the other nations.
- The pure souls will cross over it at different speeds and levels of difficulty: some will cross in the blink of an eye, some as fast as lightning, some as fast as a strong wind, and some as fast as a horse or camel. Others will walk and some will even have to crawl and hang on.
- The hypocrites will fall off the bridge and into Hell.
- The sinful believers who fall into Hell will serve their time and eventually come out once they have been purified.

Stage 5: The Final Destination

- Heaven (Jannah) is a place of Allāh's ﷻ pleasure.
- Hell (Jahannam) is a place of Allāh's ﷻ justice and wrath.
- Those entering Heaven will enter out of Allāh's ﷻ mercy.
- Those entering Hell will enter out of Allāh's ﷻ justice.

Jannah

- Jannah is where good people will go as a reward for believing in Allāh ﷻ and taking Islām as their way of life. It is for those noble people who lived a life of piety and righteousness, fulfilled their duties, obeyed Allāh's ﷻ commands and refrained from breaking His laws.
- The beauty of Jannah is beyond our imagination.
- Jannah will have palaces made from gold, silver, pearls and rubies.
- Jannah will have rivers of pure water, honey, wine and milk.
- Jannah will have provisions of all kinds.
- People can have anything they desire in Jannah.
- Jannah is a place of safety and security: no one will face any kind of harm, loss, illness or misfortune.
- Jannah is a place of happiness and joy: no one will experience fear, sorrow, grief, or discomfort.
- Nobody will die or age in Jannah.
- The people of Jannah will be allowed to see Allāh ﷻ. This will be the ultimate reward and greatest blessing.
- Jannah is an everlasting abode.
- Entry into Jannah requires effort and sacrifice. It is a place for those who lived a life of obedience by submitting to Allāh ﷻ.

Jahannam

- Jahannam is a place where Allāh ﷻ will send those that have earned His displeasure and wrath by rejecting Him and refusing to live a life of submission and obedience.
- Jahannam is a terrible place where one can neither live nor die.
- Jahannam is a place of horror and terror: there is no peace therein.
- Jahannam is a place of pain, distress and agony: there is no comfort or relief therein.
- Jahannam is a place of grief and sorrow: there is no joy therein.
- The fire of Jahannam uses stones and humans as its fuel.
- The inmates of Jahannam will be clothed in fire. Every time their skin burns, it will be replaced with fresh skin so that they can feel the pain again, in an endless cycle.
- They will be given thorny plants to eat and boiling water to drink, which will also be poured over their heads.
- The angels will whip them and venomous snakes and scorpions will be let loose on them.
- Sinful believers will eventually be released from Jahannam after they have been purified.
- The chief supervisor of Jahannam is called Mālik. He has not smiled since the time he was appointed to this position.

Questions

1. What is meant by the Final Hour and when will it occur?
2. What is meant by al-Ba'th?
3. What is meant by the Last Day?
4. What are some of the names of the Last Day?
5. What is angel Isrāfīl's ﷺ role in relation to the Final Hour and the Resurrection?
6. What are some signs that would indicate that the Last Day is close?
7. What is Barzakh and what happens there?
8. What is the Hashr and how will it be?
9. How will people collect their books of deeds?
10. What kinds of people will be allowed to do shafā'ah for others on the Day of Judgement?
11. What is the Mīzān and how does one become successful here?
12. What is Hawd al-Kawthar and what will happen here?
13. What kind of people will be driven away from the Hawd al-Kawthar?
14. What is the Sirāt?
15. How will the believers cross the Sirāt?
16. What is Jannah? Provide a description.
17. What is Jahannam? Provide a description.
18. What will happen to sinful believers?
19. How can we prepare for the Last Day?

قُلِ اللّٰهُ يُحۡيِيۡكُمۡ ثُمَّ يُمِيۡتُكُمۡ ثُمَّ يَجۡمَعُكُمۡ اِلٰى يَوۡمِ الۡقِيٰمَةِ لَا
رَيۡبَ فِيۡهِ وَلٰـكِنَّ اَكۡثَرَ النَّاسِ لَا يَعۡلَمُوۡنَ ۝

"Say, '(It is) Allāh (Who) gives you life, then causes you to die, then He will assemble you on the Day of Judgement, about which there is no doubt. But most people do not know." **(45:26)**

Chapter 6

Belief in Divine Decree

Belief in Divine Decree

Qadar means Divine Decree. It refers to the will of Allāh ﷻ and His decisions that govern His creation. The article of Qadar is related to the belief that Allāh ﷻ is the Controller of all affairs. Everything happens the way He wills or allows and nothing happens contrary to His knowledge.

The Pen and the Preserved Tablet

Before the creation of the universe, Allāh ﷻ created the Pen and commanded it to write the details of everything that will occur in the universe, from beginning to end. Through the inspiration of Allāh ﷻ, the Pen wrote down the details of every happening in accordance with the knowledge of Allāh ﷻ and His Will. This information is stored in *al-Lawh al-Mahfūz,* or the Preserved Tablet.

Thus, whatever happens in the universe happens as a result of the Will of Allāh ﷻ i.e. His permission or His tolerance for it to happen. Similarly, whatever does not happen in the universe does not happen as a result of His Will i.e. His refusal for it to happen.

This is the *Qadar* of Allāh ﷻ - the Irrevocable Decree. It is sometimes translated as fate or predestination. It does not accept addition, alteration or abrogation. It cannot be changed, overruled or undone. The Pen has been lifted and the pages have dried.

The Knowledge of Allāh ﷻ

Since the idea of Qadar is closely linked with Allāh's ﷻ attribute of knowledge, it is important to understand this attribute in detail.

The following is an outline of what we must believe about the knowledge of Allāh ﷻ:

- Allāh ﷻ is Omniscient: His knowledge is all-encompassing and absolute. It is not qualified or limited in any way. From the sounds and movements of the stars and planets to the hidden behaviours of people, plants, insects and atoms - He has total knowledge of all things.
- Allāh's ﷻ knowledge is definite, perfect and precise: It is not predicted and it can never be wrong.
- Allāh ﷻ has pre-knowledge of all happenings within His creation - His knowledge precedes everything. His knowledge of what is yet to occur is as certain as His knowledge of what has already occurred.
- Allāh's ﷻ knowledge does not increase with the unfolding of events - He already possesses all knowledge.
- Allāh ﷻ already knows how every person will use his free will, what choices he will make and what actions he will take, and to where his choices and actions will lead him.
- Every decision of Allāh ﷻ is founded upon pure knowledge and wisdom. His knowledge is His decision.

1. Creational Decree

The first type of Qadar includes those matters that Allāh ﷻ predetermined within His creation. As the Creator and Owner of everything, Allāh ﷻ does as He pleases and we are not allowed to question Him.

This type of Qadar has no connection with man's salvation or his free will.

Examples of things that fall into this category are as follows:

1. Allāh ﷻ designed the universe to operate on specific laws and constants. He predetermined the number of galaxies, stars and planets that will come into existence and when they will perish.
2. Allāh ﷻ created angels from light, jinn from fire, and mankind from clay.
3. Allāh ﷻ created various kinds of plants and animals with specific characteristics, capabilities and requirements.
4. Allāh ﷻ designed men and women differently in certain aspects of their biology.
5. Allāh ﷻ preordained the number of humans that will be born and specified how much vegetation the Earth with produce.
6. Allāh ﷻ decreed man's total life span on Earth, the amount of sustenance he shall receive, and where he shall die.

2. Worldly Decree

The second type of Qadar includes those factors that have the potential to contribute to a person's spiritual condition, both in terms of progress and decline.

Once we profess belief in Allāh ﷻ, He will test our faith in Him and in the Last Day by putting us in different circumstances and assessing our behaviour, all the while knowing how we will react. These tests will separate true believers from false ones.

Examples of things that fall into this category are as follows:

Prosperity	**Adversity**
Wealth	Poverty
Health	Sickness
Success	Failure
Gain	Loss
Ease	Difficulty

- Allāh ﷻ decides who should face what kind of fate (test) in this world, when he should face it, and how much of it he should face.
- How we wish to react to fate is entirely up to us, though Allāh ﷻ already knows about what choices we will make, what actions we will take, and the consequences this will lead us to.

Summary

1. All worldly fate, good and bad, is predestined by Allāh ﷻ.
2. Interpreting worldly fate as good or bad is based on an individual's perception of it and personal conduct with it.

⇒ **Example 1:** Sickness and misfortune may be seen as bad things in the sense that there comes with it much pain and inconvenience. Yet, they can also be seen as good things from another perspective. Consider our immune system: it cannot learn how to fight infections if we don't fall ill. Similarly, a person who has never experienced misfortune and hardship cannot understand the suffering of others. These things are beneficial and necessary for our personal development. It is by experiencing adversity that we can truly appreciate prosperity.

⇒ **Example 2:** Wealth can be seen as something good in the sense that it allows a person to enjoy life and help others. However, not everyone will use their wealth to do good. People who are selfish and greedy will be consumed and blinded by their love of wealth if they don't manage their money matters in accordance with the Sharī'ah. This would eventually lead them to abusing wealth, neglecting their duties, violating the rights of others, and an endless list of corruption and immorality. So wealth is not so good for everyone after all. It may be a blessing for one but a calamity for another.

3. Allāh سُبْحَانَهُ وَتَعَالَى knows best about what is good for us and what is bad for us. He is the Best of Planners, the All-Knowing.
4. Allāh سُبْحَانَهُ وَتَعَالَى decides to whom and how a test should be given. He will test people differently, yet fairly.
5. The real good and bad fate is not the fate we are tested with, but the consequences in which we land ourselves through the choices we make and actions we take.
6. The worldly life was created as a means of testing man's faith. Like any test, the tests of faith will also come in ways we did not imagine and moments we did not expect.
7. Those who respond to their tests appropriately and act according to the law and guidance of Allāh سُبْحَانَهُ وَتَعَالَى will get closer to Allāh سُبْحَانَهُ وَتَعَالَى. They will be rewarded generously and their faith will be protected and strengthened.
8. Those who respond to their tests inappropriately and act against the law and guidance of Allāh سُبْحَانَهُ وَتَعَالَى will fail the intended test and lose out on the rewards that could have been theirs. They will become distant from Allāh سُبْحَانَهُ وَتَعَالَى and their faith will become weak.
9. Allāh سُبْحَانَهُ وَتَعَالَى already knows how each individual will respond to his or her tests and what end result they would lead to.
10. Allāh سُبْحَانَهُ وَتَعَالَى can save a person from taking the wrong course of action and from making the wrong choices. His divine intervention can be attained:
    - Through His sheer mercy.
    - If a person truly seeks His help.

Our Behaviour

1. We should believe that all good and bad is from Allāh ﷾.
2. We should ask Allāh ﷾ to allow us to act appropriately in every situation, in accordance with His law and guidance, and always keep in mind that the power to do good and the ability to refrain from evil comes only from Him.
3. We should respond to good fate with gratitude and bad fate with patience and prayer.
4. We should counter any misfortune that befalls us or anyone else with goodness and virtue.
5. We should believe that He knows of our condition, He is watching our response and is also aware of its outcome.
6. We should keep our faith in Allāh ﷾ and trust that He knows best. He is the most Wise. He is the Controller of all affairs. He is the One Who answers the call of the distressed, removes calamities and appreciates good.
7. We should remember Allāh ﷾ and call unto Him in times of prosperity and in times of adversity.
8. We should find ease in knowing that what is meant for us will never miss us, and what misses us was never meant for us.
9. We should ask Allāh ﷾ to help us in all our affairs, as He intervenes if His help is sought with faith and sincerity.
10. We should not be so concerned about what kind of test we are given as much as we should be about how we respond to that test and the consequence it will lead us to.

3. Final Decree

The third type of Qadar is directly related to the issue of salvation, that is saving oneself from Hell and earning entry in to Heaven by bringing faith in Allāh ﷻ and submitting to Him. This is where much confusion and error has occurred.

Many people have misunderstood Qadar to mean that man's eternal salvation or damnation is predestined by Allāh ﷻ in the sense that He enters them into one of the two by way of forced acceptance or rejection of the Truth, without them having the ability to act according to their own will and choice.

No Compulsion in Religion

Know that Allāh ﷻ does not force anyone into accepting or rejecting Him, neither does He allow someone to compel another to do the same. The glorious Qur'ān clearly states that there is no compulsion in religion. Guidance has been made clear from misguidance. A person can either choose to believe or disbelieve.

If Allāh ﷻ willed, He could have easily compelled all His subjects to believe and surrender to Him. But that would defeat the purpose of the worldly test, and man would not be entitled to reward or deserving of punishment in the Hereafter. In Islām, it is clear that man will be judged based on the beliefs he holds and the actions he does with his own free will.

Free Will

Allāh ﷻ willed that man should have his own free will, with which he chooses his faith, actions, and way of life. Allāh ﷻ permitted man to determine his own fate in the Afterlife and earn his abode. He gave man the understanding of good and bad, showed him the ways, both right and wrong, and made truth distinct from falsehood. He scattered signs that reflect His existence and truth in the universe and within man himself, which the sound intellect ('aql) would recognise, and which the natural disposition (fitrah) would accept. He also sent Messengers as warners and guides.

Allāh ﷻ tolerated the fact that by giving man the ability to exercise his own choice, many would choose to reject Him, thereby earning His wrath and being damned into Hell. Out of His mercy, He kept the door of supplication, repentance and reform open, so that should any soul realise the truth and sincerely seek to be helped or rescued, then the Merciful Lord would help him and take him out of the darkness of rejection (kufr) and into the light of monotheism (tawhīd).

Allāh ﷻ already knows the choices that each man will make and his final destination. He knows who will seek His guidance and who will remain arrogant. His knowledge of how man will use his free will, however, does not influence man's free will; it only reflects what will definitely occur.

DIVINE DECREE

CREATIONAL DECREE	WORLDLY DECREE	FINAL DECREE
Allāh's Will within His Creation	Allāh's Selection of Tests for His Servants	Allāh's Knowledge of Man's Final Destination
Universal Laws of Nature	Affluence	Salvation - Admission into Jannah
Universal Design	Poverty	Damnation - Admission into Jahannam
Universal Mechanisms	Health	
Creation of Various Different Creatures and Plants	Sickness	
	Prosperity	
	Adversity	

Questions

1. What is the meaning of Qadar?
2. What is the meaning of 'al-Lawh al-Mahfūz', and what does it contain?
3. What do Muslims believe about Allāh's سبحانه وتعالى knowledge?
4. If Allāh سبحانه وتعالى had already decided the final fate of each and every person, how is it fair for those who will end up in Hell?
5. What is meant by 'Creational Decree'? Explain your answer using some examples.
6. What is meant by 'Worldly Decree'? Give some examples.
7. How should a believer respond to Worldly Decree?
8. What is meant by 'Final Decree'?
9. What is free will and why did Allāh سبحانه وتعالى give it to mankind?
10. Why does Allāh سبحانه وتعالى not allow forcing people into Islām?

Chapter 7

Faith Fortified

The Value of Faith

Faith in Allāh ﷻ is the most valuable asset man can possess. It is the key to salvation. Shaytān is constantly making effort to strip us of our Īmān or corrupt it in some way or another. Thus, believers must make every effort to protect their Īmān.

How to Protect Our faith

1. One way to strengthen and protect our Īmān is through continuous reflection over the Islamic beliefs (creed). The more one reads about Allāh ﷻ and the Last Day, the more clarity and strength one will gain. Therefore, make it a practice to study the glorious Qur'ān and the life and teachings of the holy Prophet ﷺ.
2. Another way to protect our faith is by adopting taqwā. Taqwā means to fear the displeasure of Allāh ﷻ, and to protect oneself from earning it by obeying and heeding His law. Taqwā is a protective guard from spiritual harm. By adopting taqwā, one is able to strengthen his faith and protect it from Shaytān.

How to Attain Taqwā

Taqwā is attained by obeying Allāh ﷻ and His Messenger ﷺ, in other words, by following the glorious Qur'ān in accordance with the Sunnah of the holy Prophet ﷺ. Taqwā is the product and result of true submission and obedience, which is the essence of Islām.

The Importance of Islām

Imām Abū Ja'far at-Tahāwī ﷺ states:

مَا سَلِمَ فِي دِيْنِهِ إِلَّا مَنْ سَلَّمَ لِلّٰهِ عَزَّ وَجَلَّ، وَلِرَسُوْلِهِ... وَلَا تَثْبُتُ قَدَمُ الْإِسْلَامِ إِلَّا عَلٰى ظَهْرِ التَّسْلِيْمِ وَالْاِسْتِسْلَامِ

"No one is secure in his religion unless he submits himself to Allāh ﷻ and His Messenger ﷺ and one's footing in Islām is not firm except on the ground of submission and surrender."

1. While Īmān is religious belief, Islām is religious practice.
2. The sacred law of Allāh ﷻ, otherwise known as the Sharī'ah, consists of commands, prohibitions and advice. Allāh ﷻ requires the believers to adhere to this law if they truly believe in Him and love Him.
3. The Sharī'ah seeks to regulate our thoughts, intentions, beliefs, desires, emotions, actions, speech and character, so that our lives are lived in a way that pleases Allāh ﷻ.
4. The essence of submission to Allāh ﷻ is to abstain from all forms of disobedience to Him i.e. from sinful and offensive acts. Any act that is committed contrary to His command or prohibition is counted as disobedience.
5. The source of the Sharī'ah is the Qur'ān and Sunnah.
6. Observance of the Sharī'ah is called Islām (submission).
7. Allāh ﷻ tests the truth and quality of our faith by testing the level of our obedience to Him.

8. A person's religious practice serves as an evidence of his faith. Without this, anyone can claim to believe in Allāh ﷻ and the Last Day.
9. The one whose faith in Allāh ﷻ and the Last Day is true will readily conform to the guidance of the Qur'ān and Sunnah, avoiding its prohibitions and fulfilling its commands as much as possible. He will make sacrifices for the pleasure of Allāh ﷻ, and will hold His pleasure to be more dear than anything else. He will not make excuses or consider himself above the law of Allāh ﷻ.
10. The one whose faith in Allāh ﷻ and the Last Day is false or weak will neglect the guidance of the Qur'ān and Sunnah. He will follow his sinful desires and give preference to his own will over the will of Allāh ﷻ. He will find excuses to avoid practicing the Sharī'ah, yet he will expect to attain salvation because he was a 'believer' by word.
11. Obedience to Allāh ﷻ helps us get closer to Him and increases the quality of our faith, while disobedience to Allāh ﷻ moves us away from Him and reduces the quality of our faith.
12. The one who is mindful of the Sharī'ah is blessed and guided towards further goodness, while the lawbreaker is deprived of divine enablement and inspiration.
13. The strength of true Īmān powers the growth of one's Islām. Through sincere and continuous practice, one

eventually reaches the stage of Ihsān, which is when the true knowledge of tawhīd (monotheism) is unveiled and one reaches a state of spiritual harmony.

14. When a person's Islām matures, Allāh ﷻ multiplies his rewards and overlooks his mistakes.
15. Allāh ﷻ loves those who strive to perfect their faith and practice, and for them He opens up multiple paths and opportunities of success.
16. A person is either in a state of spiritual prosperity by choice or in a state of spiritual decline by default.
17. In order to become spiritually prosperous and save oneself from spiritual decline, one must make practical effort.
18. If our faith is followed by sincere practice according to the Sunnah, and we surrender to Allāh ﷻ and persevere in His service, then our faith will be safe and it will also grow from strength to strength.
19. Every door has a key, and every key has its teeth. A key with no teeth or faulty teeth will not open a door. Īmān is the key to Jannah and Islām is its teeth.
20. We must always remember that our faith will be judged according to our practice. Therefore, we must never be deceived into thinking that our verbal affirmation of Īmān is sufficient without practice. A person whose faith is void of practical conformity is in grave danger of losing it at the time of death.

In a famous hadīth (prophetic saying), the holy Prophet ﷺ gave the example of Īmān with that of [a tree with] branches. Let's analyse this impressive example in some detail.

The Pure Seed of Tawhīd

The seed of a tree is hidden in pure soil. If the seed finds the right conditions to survive, its root breaks through to form a trunk. Similarly, the seed of tawhīd is ingrained in man's natural disposition (fitrah), by which he recognises his Creator. If it is well nurtured, it will bring forth the trunk of Īmān.

Īmān - The Trunk of Spirituality

A tree survives through the support and supply of its trunk. Without a trunk, there is no tree , let alone any leaf, fruit, or shade. Similarly, Īmān is the trunk of spirituality. It powers and guides the soul and disciplines the ego. Without Īmān, true spirituality simply cannot exist or thrive.

Islām - The Test and Proof of Īmān

A tree trunk without branches cannot mature, that is, it cannot grow leaves or bear fruit. With no branches, a tree is also exposed to danger and risks survival.

Good deeds are like the branches of a tree trunk. If one's Īmān is healthy, it will manifest in the form of good deeds. The purer one's Īmān, the greater his good deeds will be in quality and number. Without these deeds, our Imān is at risk.

Ihsān - The Maturity of Īmān

A tree matures when its branches grow leaves and bear fruit. The healthier the tree, the more branches it will sprout, and the healthier and tastier its fruits will be. More branches mean more benefit—more leaves, more shade, more fruit and more beauty.

Similarly, the more observant we are of the laws of Islām, the better our chances of being able to attain taqwā. Our Īmān matures and reaches different heights when our Islām is strong enough to generate taqwā within us. This stage of maturity is known as Ihsān. When a person reaches this stage, his faith is anchored and secured from the attacks of Shaytān.

Shaytān's first attack is always on a person's Īmān, which he will try to snatch or corrupt in some way or another. If he fails on this, his next step will be to attack one's Islām, making every effort to divert them away from obeying Allāh ﷻ, as that is the evidence and shield of Īmān. Once he succeeds in removing a person's shield, his attack on his Īmān becomes easy. Therefore, in order to protect our **Īmān**, and be able to reach the stage of **Ihsān**, we must take great care of our **Islām**.

Hereunder is a list of practical branches that can help you guard your Imān and steer it towards maturity.

Branches of Īmān

1. To believe in Allāh, love Him and obey Him.
2. To fear Allāh's punishment and displeasure.
3. To have hope in the mercy of Allāh.
4. To place one's trust in Allāh.
5. To be mindful of Allāh.
6. To love and honour the Messenger of Allāh.
7. To follow the teachings and practice of the Messenger ﷺ.
8. To love the Companions of the Messenger of Allāh.
9. To love the righteous slaves of Allāh.
10. To love and despise for the sake of Allāh.
11. To find good deeds desirable and bad deeds detestable.
12. To feel joy over doing good deeds and remorse upon committing bad deeds.
13. To seek forgiveness from Allāh upon committing a sin.
14. To act with sincerity in everything.
15. To seek knowledge of the religion.
16. To pass on knowledge and spread the message of Islām.
17. To recite the glorious Qur'ān, listen to it being recited, reflect over its meanings, and practice upon its teachings.
18. To turn to Allāh in du'ā (supplication).
19. To engage in the dhikr of Allāh.
20. To maintain cleanliness and purity.
21. To offer the five daily prayers with punctuality.
22. To observe the fasts of Ramadhān.

23. To pay one's zakāt and fulfil all financial obligations.
24. To perform the hajj and 'umrah.
25. To carry out optional prayers, fasts and charity.
26. To encourage and assist in good deeds.
27. To refrain from encouraging or assisting in sinful deeds.
28. To have good will and care for the creation.
29. To desire for others what one desires for oneself, and dislike for others what one dislikes for oneself.
30. To behave appropriately at all times with everyone.
31. To have a good opinion of others.
32. To ensure the safety of others from one's harm.
33. To conceal the sins of others and protect their dignity.
34. To abstain from criticising or finding faults in others.
35. To refrain from all kinds of oppression and injustice.
36. To reconcile between people and solve their problems.
37. To greet those who you know and do not know.
38. To be good with one's parents, spouse and children.
39. To fulfil one's responsibilities and the rights of others.
40. To maintain ties of kinship and be good to one's relatives.
41. To maintain good relations with one's friends.
42. To be good to one's neighbours.
43. To take care of those under one's care and authority.
44. To take care of the poor, the weak and the vulnerable.
45. To fulfil the rights of the deceased.
46. To visit the sick.
47. To honour the guest.

48. To assist the traveller/foreigner.
49. To be kind and generous.
50. To express gratitude upon a blessing.
51. To exercise patience upon a calamity.
52. To be content with whatever Allāh ﷾ has given you.
53. To shun the love and desire for the world.
54. To adopt humility and shun arrogance and vanity.
55. To refrain from malice, hatred and jealousy.
56. To refrain from getting angry or acting upon impulse.
57. To abstain from swearing and cursing.
58. To abstain from being rude and offensive.
59. To avoid backbiting.
60. To avoid slander.
61. To eat halāl foods and refrain from harām foods.
62. To act with moderation in one's affairs.
63. To ensure that one's income is pure.
64. To refrain from devouring the property of others.
65. To spend money in the right causes.
66. To repay any loans and debts owed to others.
67. To keep the trust of one who entrusts you.
68. To be just and fair in all one's dealings and judgements.
69. To fulfil one's oaths and promises.
70. To abstain from dishonesty, fraud, and cheating.
71. To be chaste and protect oneself from immorality.
72. To wear modest and appropriate clothing.
73. To take care of the Earth and the environment.

Prayers of the Faithful

Prayer 1:

ٱلۡحَمۡدُ لِلَّهِ ٱلَّذِي هَدَىٰنَا لِهَٰذَا وَمَا كُنَّا لِنَهۡتَدِيَ لَوۡلَآ أَنۡ هَدَىٰنَا ٱللَّهُ

"All praise is for Allāh Who guided us to this (Faith). And we would never have been guided had Allāh not guided us." (7:43)

Prayer 2:

رَبَّنَا لَا تُزِغۡ قُلُوبَنَا بَعۡدَ إِذۡ هَدَيۡتَنَا وَهَبۡ لَنَا مِن لَّدُنكَ رَحۡمَةًۚ إِنَّكَ أَنتَ ٱلۡوَهَّابُ

"Our Lord, do not cause our hearts to deviate or stray after You have guided us, and grant us mercy from Your own. Indeed, You are the Great Giver." (3:8)

Prayer 3:

رَبَّنَآ ءَاتِنَا مِن لَّدُنكَ رَحۡمَةً وَهَيِّئۡ لَنَا مِنۡ أَمۡرِنَا رَشَدًا

"Our Lord, grant us mercy from Yourself and arrange for us the right guidance for our affairs." (18:10)

Prayer 4:

رَبِّ أَوۡزِعۡنِيٓ أَنۡ أَشۡكُرَ نِعۡمَتَكَ ٱلَّتِيٓ أَنۡعَمۡتَ عَلَيَّ وَعَلَىٰ وَٰلِدَيَّ وَأَنۡ أَعۡمَلَ صَٰلِحًا تَرۡضَىٰهُ

وَأَدۡخِلۡنِي بِرَحۡمَتِكَ فِي عِبَادِكَ ٱلصَّٰلِحِينَ

"My Lord, enable me to be grateful for Your favours that You have bestowed upon me and my parents, and to do good deeds that You approve of, and admit me by Your mercy into (the ranks of) Your righteous servants." (27:19)

Prayer 5:

اَللّٰهُمَّ اٰتِ نَفْسِيْ تَقْوَاهَا، وَزَكِّهَا أَنْتَ خَيْرُ مَنْ زَكَّاهَا، أَنْتَ وَلِيُّهَا وَمَوْلَاهَا

"O Allāh, give my soul its (shield of) taqwā; and purify it - You are the One Who is best at purifying it; You are its Protector and its Guardian." (Muslim)

Prayer 6:

يَا مُقَلِّبَ الْقُلُوْبِ، ثَبِّتْ قَلْبِيْ عَلٰى دِيْنِكَ

"O Turner of hearts, fix our hearts upon Your religion." (Tirmidhī)

Prayer 7:

اَللّٰهُمَّ اهْدِنِيْ وَسَدِّدْنِيْ

"O Allāh, guide me and rectify me." (Muslim)

Prayer 8:

اَللّٰهُمَّ إِنِّيْ أَسَأَلُكَ إِيْمَانًا لَا يَرْتَدُّ، وَنَعِيْمًا لَا يَنْفَدُ، وَمُرَافَقَةَ النَّبِيِّ فِيْ أَعْلٰى غُرَفِ الْجَنَّةِ، جَنَّةِ الْخُلْدِ.

"O Allāh, I ask You for such faith that does not deviate or stray, and such blessings that do not end, and the company of the Prophet in the highest chambers of Paradise, in the Garden of Eternity." (Ahmad)

Questions

1. Why is Shaytān always trying to take our Īmān away?
2. What things should a believer do to protect his Īmān?
3. What is the meaning of Islām?
4. How is submission to Allāh ﷻ a sign of true faith?
5. Why is practicing Islām (submission to Allāh by adhering to His law) so important? And how does it benefit one's faith?
6. What is the meaning of Ihsān, and how does one reach this level?
7. Why is the example of Īmān said to be like that of a tree trunk, and why is Islām (actions) said to be similar to the branches of a tree?
    i. When do these branches begin to shoot out from the trunk and grow?
    ii. When do the branches begin to grow leaves and give fruit?
8. If Shaytān fails to take your Īmān away directly, what will his next course of action be? What will he attack next and why do you think he will do that?
9. From the list of the branches of Īmān, identify 10 branches of faith that you are practicing in your life. How can you improve them?
10. Identify 10 branches of faith that you are not currently practicing, but would like to bring them into your practice soon. What steps can you take to achieve this?

Notes

Best of Stories
Sūrah Yūsuf is more than just a story of one of our beloved Prophets ﷺ, there much wisdom and lessons to be learnt and understood. All the knowledge com from our honourable Shaykh, inspiration and Ustādh, Shaykh Mufti Saiful Islā Sāhib. May Allāh ﷻ shower Mufti Sāhib with mercy and accept the day in, day o effort he carries out in the work of Dīn. **UK RRP:£4:00**

Call of Nuh
For 950 years, Sayyidunā Nūh ﷺ persevered night and day in continuous succession in preaching the message; unwavering and relentless in his mission. Not once did he feel that his calling was in vain. He stood firm and resolute in continuing with the mission that he was sent with, in proclaiming the message of the oneness of Allāh ﷻ; year after year, decade upon decade, century after century, but this failed to convince the people of the truth. **UK RRP:£4:00**

Ready for Judgement Day?
For those that doubt the Day of Resurrection, Allāh ﷻ is reaffirming that there is no scope for uncertainty; this day is indisputable and will surely occur. The day when the truth will be laid out bare and everything will be exposed, there will be no place to flee or escape to. Regretting that day will be of no avail; excuses will fail to safeguard or shelter a person from breaking free and escaping judgement. **UK RRP:£4:00**

Flee Towards Allāh ﷻ
Sūrah Al-Ma'ārij begins by addressing the disbelievers who used to mock the Holy Prophet ﷺ about the Day of Judgement. In this Surah, Allāh ﷻ severely reproaches those who deny it assuming that there is only one life; the life of this world. The Sūrah manifests its horrors and catastrophic scenes that the entire creation shall witness on that very day. Mankind will then realise that on this horrific day, they will be judged by their own actions. **UK RRP:£4:00**

A Glimpse of Paradise

Time is the true wealth we have at our disposal though it cannot be amassed. The only way we can utilise it to our advantage is when we do righteous deeds and actions; for this will act in our favour in the Ākhirah (Hereafter). These moments will be preserved in exchange for moments of greater happiness and bliss in the next life. Therefore, we need to perform righteous deeds and actions in the short duration of time we have at our disposal in this temporary worldly life. **UK RRP:£4:00**

Living Islām in Modern Times

This book is a compilation of various articles written by Shaykh Dr. Rafāqat Rashīd Sāhib in the popular Al-Mu'min Magazine. Considering the great benefit these articles will bring to the Ummah, Mufti Saiful Islām Sāhib decided to edit and transform them into a book format, making the content easily accessible for readers. **UK RRP:£4:00**

Lanterns of Knowledge

Once the commentary of Kitābul 'Ilm in Bukhāri was completed, we realised that this chapter is an entire topic in itself due to its fascinating and insightful perspective on knowledge. When compiling this commentary, there were many beautiful reminders as well as points of guidance for everyone's personal life as well as their lifelong quest for knowledge. Therefore, the commentary of this chapter alone would be beneficial for all seekers of knowledge and the idea of publishing it as a separate book came to mind. **UK RRP:£10:00**

A CLEAR VICTORY

This book "A Clear Victory" is an enlightening commentary of Sūrah Al-Fath. It is cited in Sahīh Al-Bukhāri regarding the virtue of this Sūrah that Sayyidunā Umar Ibn Al-Khattāb ﷺ reported that the Messenger of Allāh ﷺ said: "This night a Sūrah was sent down to me that is more beloved to me than all what the sun shines over," then he read, *"We have indeed accorded a triumph to you, a manifest triumph, indeed"*. **UK RRP:£5:00**

BLURB – A Day with the Prophet ﷺ
This treatise before you is a collection of the daily Prophetic Sunnats - practices and ha guide for us all to follow. The objective behind this book is to instil the love for the Pro by encouraging our readers to implement his Sunnats into their daily lives. The daily S range from worship to general social and personal etiquettes and conduct. Each habit to a specific Sunnah is referenced from a hadīth. On the face of it, it may appear overwh but I can assure you that once you start to slowly implement them, then overtime they g ly become your secondary nature. Each Sunnat is never difficult to adopt for a true b
UK RRP £5.00

BLURB – Beware of Hypocrisy
The Munāfiqūn (hypocrites) were a group of people who did not have the courage to openly oppose the holy Prophet ﷺ feeling that it would be unfavourable in their favour if they wished to find a way of overpowering the Muslims. They felt that they had to wait for the right moment and opportunity to present itself before they made their move, and this is what we witness throughout the course of action they took. Allāh ﷻ then revealed verses alerting the believers in unveiling the truth about their presence and the hypocrisy they concealed within their hearts. **UK RRP £3.00**

BLURB – Divorce in Islām
The sacred law of Islām is a complete and chaste system of life. The proper functioning of human race depends on the proper maintenance of marital relationship. Islām has focused attention on family issues most exhaustively. By a careful analysis of the holy Qurān, we notice that commercial contracts like sale, partnership, hiring and so on are though among the most important socio-economic matters, the holy Qurān has restricted itself to setting down their basic principles, and the bye-laws are rarely ever touched upon. **UK RRP**

BLURB – Mind Your Own Business
This book is a gateway towards understanding how to live a sharīʿah-compliant life in business. By adhering to these guidelines, you are sure to attract the blessings of Allāh ﷻ in this world and the Hereafter, and live a life of true happiness and contentment.The lessons included in it are not just to be read, but to be lived. And that must start today. Not tomorrow. Not next year. Today. **UK RRP £4.00**

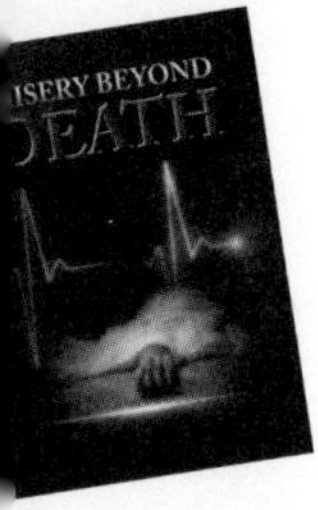

BLURB - Misery Beyond Death

One of the aspects which differentiates a Muslim from a non-Muslim is the belief in the Ākhirah (Hereafter). Muslims believe that they will be held accountable for wrongdoings and rewarded for good. This is the core aspect of the message in the holy Qur'ān to which Allāh ﷻ draws our attention throughout so that we believe in Him. In reinforcing this message, Allāh ﷻ describes extensively the scenes of the Day of Judgement. **UK RRP £4.00**

.URB – Muslim Guide to Pandemics

›erson will face many different challenges throughout their life. However, the beauty of Islām ; in the mere fact that it has all the answers to every possible situation. A Muslim may be strug- ıg to cope, yet the holy Qur'ān and ahādīth are filled with antidotes to these struggles. As Mus- ıs, we are encouraged to view our calamities as blessings. More so, it is an opportunity for us to n to Allāh ﷻ with a sincere heart and strengthen our īmān (faith). **UK RRP £4.00**

BLURB – Watch your Character

In this Sūrah, Allāh ﷻ defended the holy Prophet ﷺ of his elevated rank as being raised to a position of great spiritual dignity, ingrained in the very fundamental structure of his being, which moulded him with a disposition and temperament far greater than that of any being to have ever existed. Sūrah Qalam also teaches us to inculcate good habits and shun aside all bad habits. **UK RRP £5.00**

URB – The World of Jinns

s is full of references to the holy Qur'ān and hadīth, exploring and providing insight into this ıtion which we have little knowledge about. We will find much theories on this creation which only speculative and baseless. Here, we can be assured that this information is genuine and hentic, knowledge which has been revealed to us by Allāh ﷻ through the medium of his be- ed Prophet ﷺ. **UK RRP £4.00**

BLURB – Actions Speak Louder than Words

Sūrah As-Saff teaches us some fundamental ways of how to live our lives as believers and not be deceived by the materialistic things of this worldly life. In order to achieve this, we can take inspiration by looking at the lives of the Sahābah ﷺ and our pious predecessors. They were firm in acting upon the things they would preach. We need to keep in mind that when we remain true to our pledge, then Allāh ﷻ will allow us to remain dominant over everyone else. **UK RRP £3.00**